SCIENCE AND TECHNOLOGY IN INDIA'S TRANSFORMATION

SCIENCE AND TECHNOLOGY IN INDIA'S TRANSFORMATION

J.N. NANDA

CONCEPT PUBLISHING COMPANY, NEW DELHI

First Published 1986

J.N. Nanda (*b*. 1920-)

Published by

Naurang Rai
Concept Publishing Company
H-13, Bali Nagar
NEW DELHI-110015 (India)

Printed in India by

Printway India
at S. Narayan & Sons
7117/13, Pahari Dhiraj,
DELHI-110006

Dedicated
To
My Wife

FOREWORD

It is a pleasure to write a foreword for the book on "Science and Technology in India's Transformation" by Dr. J.N. Nanda. The analysis done by Dr. J.N. Nanda is timely.

Ignorance, superstition, lack of initiative and mismanagement are major reasons for backwardness and poverty. A scientific and rational approach and a proper value system can redeem the future of the vast majority of the people of this country. Dr. Nanda has made several useful suggestions for the betterment of our society. He has dealt with problems of communalism, unemployment and inefficiency. Many of his suggestions are practical and can be given effect to without amending existing legislation and within our institutional mechanisms. I hope that this book will be studied seriously by scientists, planners, administrators and others interested in development.

C.N.R. Rao
President
Indian National
Science Academy

PREFACE

WHEN India was a British colony and the many gifts of the British rule were taught in school, the author realised that the most valuable contribution of the white man who bore the burden of an enslaved people was the example of patriotic hard work and of modern organization and technology. The indigenous poverty, dirt and laziness, wasteful gossip and back-biting, religious bigotry, looking down on labour and preoccupation with short-sighted self-interest were visible everywhere. Still, there were some oases of sacrifice and service. Mahatma Gandhi's name was heard everywhere. In the Punjab, a reformist Arya Samaj was active in the uplift of untouchables and in the field of education especially of girls. Slowly it dawned on the author that the entire country was in a ferment because of the juxtaposition of European scholarship and imported science and technology with the Indian mind.

Gandhi and Nehru and innumerable freedom fighters not only struggled for freedom but also worked for the awakening of the country to its heritage and to its unbroken destiny. On independence the major problems facing the country were still the decadence grown during caste slavery, feudal tyranny and colonial domination. People had to be trained afresh in initiative and made alive to the need and the use of better tools. The semi-literate bigots brought about regional and communal conflicts and language riots and thus wasted precious time and resources required urgently for national reconstruction and development. Armed conflicts provoked by external enemies also interfered but brought home further to the nation that security also depended entirely on getting ahead in modern science and technology with or without the assistance of others. A strong India was not welcome everywhere since she was already vociferous in challenging injustice and exploitation anywhere. With the vision of Indian leadership and the hard work of few dedicated people belonging to the generations that had experienced bondage, India has survived many challenges with credit. Now under the stewardship of Rajiv Gandhi, India is diligently tackling the fundamental problems of narrowness of outlook and widespread poverty. In these tasks the recourse must be to the scientific approach and better production tools. There has to be abundant supply of power, of machines and skills. India already has had considerable success in harnessing science and technology along with cooperative management techniques to agriculture. Many new avenues of employment are opening with the spread of new technologies and skills like nuclear technology, computer and information technology and the advent of tailored materials. The transformation of India is happening before our eyes. Scientific value judgements for the welfare of humanity can alone bring about stability in human affairs. There are still many tasks to be done. Still a large part of the population lives below the poverty line. Fundamentalism, a harsh reality for division, is raising its ugly head here and there. India has not yet evolved a universal language for science and technology in which all Indians at least can understand and discuss new advances. The ideals of simplicity and sacrifice are becoming dim under the onslaught of consumerism prevalent in certain technically advanced countries and the misguided modernism of some of the otherwise well meaning media and the short sighted advertisement policies.

This is the right time for a moment of weighing all aspects of the ongoing transformation. This kind of comprehensive grasp of the Indian reality is not an easy task and one can easily provoke criticism and controversy from the specialists who may have studied very deeply one of the many facets of the Indian scene and its evolution. The author has made bold to carry out this task for the thinking public of the developing countries so that they become aware of the many issues involved and can press for right priorities. India's transformation can be educative for many developing countries that cherish democracy, human dignity and security along with the banishment of poverty. There must be a rigorous method for monitoring the planned progress and for checking if the benefits are not being denied to the common man. There is need for a planned basic consumerism which denies ostentatious living but creates demand for universal work for profit.

The author has dealt in detail with possible shortcomings in the development process that might delay the achievement of desired results and he has scattered many suggestions from experiences within the country and abroad which can be built upon by the planners and managers in a developing society. He hopes that the technocrats and the political heavywights who often initiate trends for progress will receive this small effort with appreciation and find it useful, in the tremendous task of transformation of their developing countries.

The author is grateful to many eminent friends who were shown the initial manuscript and who often gave him useful suggestions and encouraged him. He should especially mention among them Dr. B. Bhatia, Dr. A.R. Kidwai, Dr. B.D. Nagchaudhury, Dr. S.Z. Qasim, Dr. M.S. Randhawa, and Shri Tarlok Singh.

J.N. NANDA

CONTENTS

1

INTRODUCTION

FEW events have influenced world history as profoundly as the winning of freedom by India in 1947 A.D. This was the beginning of the end of colonialism. The non-violent victorious struggle for freedom became an inspiration for others. The blacks in the United States and the oppressed everywhere rose in protest and waged heroic struggles. The reformation and renaissance that had started in India during the period of foreign domination found its full expression after freedom. Obscurantism in the guise of religious superiority complex was responsible for the formation of Pakistan where it could play with the destinies of own votaries. The excesses of communal and feudal reaction in free India are facing the might of secular democracy and are in retreat.

In free India there have been revolutionary changes in all aspects of people's lives. Mahatma Gandhi and his futuristic doctrines based on the age-old philosophy and spirit of India were the product of his times. A most pertinent change agent was the juxtaposition of the British way of life and work, and the Indian scene. The nineteenth century and the 17th century got mixed up as in a laboratory reaction vessel. The catalyst was modern science and technology and not the religious or political thought alien to India. In traditional technology, India was in most ways ahead of the Europeans when the control of India slipped over to the British in 1757 at Plassey. The British spread, albeit at a slow pace, modern science, technology and management on the Indian sub-continent. Great scholars and scientists from Europe contributed in this and many Indian reformers and revolutionaries learnt from them. Along with the introduction to modern science and technology, India also reawakened to the ancient store of knowledge within India rediscovered by European zeal.

In India there were layers of ritualistic beliefs and cobwebs of superstition. The basic humanist tenets of Hindu thought could be refurbished now by the reformers. Mahatma Gandhi and Jawaharlal Nehru culminating in a long list of enlightened leaders re-established secularism and humanism. Nehru placed scientific socialism, as paramount in social and political thought in the country. A developed society must have rule of law, democratic rights, economic well-being and cooperative living. All these values are now enshrined in the constitution and the guiding principles of free India. The husbanding of national resources and increased industrial and agricultural production, better means of communication, and internal and external security are best developed by harnessing science and technology. It is only the modern technological developments that provide hope of continuing expansion of production outstripping the increase in population. Scientific solutions to psychological, social and economic problems alone raise hopes of a world community living in peace and plenty.

The political, social and economic organization of the modern civilization depends on the technology and industry evolved from physics and chemistry. The analogies provided by modern science also simplify the understanding of spiritual speculations. Scientific attitude alone allows progress since there is no authority standing in the way of new facts and fresh theories. Human progress has been tied to progress in his tools. Better tools are the product of advances in science and technology.

India is an epitome of the whole world. From ancient times she has striven for unity in diversity. If India succeeds in the task of development along with democratic freedom, there will be hope for the world. India is sharpening the value system that will assure survival of mankind.

Anticipation, planning and innovation are the steps that can feed, clothe and house the billions through better technology, new knowledge and new management methods. The Indian ideal of evenness of temper, feeling of kinship with nature, plants and animals have now the stamp of science for environment of peace and abundance. Future will bring about many unimagined opportunities for the skillful use of human ingenuity and creativity. New education and fresh opportunities for the unfolding of the talents of the common people of India is producing a flowering not dreamt of before.

Prof. Eugene P. Wigner has stressed an extremly important role of science of providing ever-lasting goals of enquiry that may be striven for. The comprehension of the fundamentals of nature that underscore the behaviour of reality is the key to universal progress. According to Lawrence Bragg, the essence of science lies not in discovering facts but in discovering new ways of thinking about them.

This book reviews the changes that are occurring in India and offers suggestions for accelerating them towards full employment, and better life for the people. The scientific contribution to internal and external security is also discussed. These pages are addressed to students of history and political science as well as to politicians and planners. The experience in the application of the scientific approach for solving national problems in India and for promoting international understanding will be useful also to other developing countries. The problems of lack of hygiene, poverty, inefficiency and bias are endemic in struggling societies. Science education, entrepreunership and humanist outlook would overcome these difficulties.

The reader may find it convenient to first have a look at the contents for the organisation of the material presented in this book. In the two chapters that follow, the Indian social and economic conditions before and after independence are outlined. Next three chapters deal with the march of science and technology in the country. There is an interlude, chapter VII, describing the current conditions. The next two chapters again take up the major theme of interaction of science and technology towards the major goals of society in India, and the steps that might promote science and technology for the development of the country. A concluding chapter deals with current problems and suitable action based on scientific approach of secularism and democracy.

The author is indebted to his teachers and colleagues in the many institutions he has worked for enabling him to form this assessment that has been penned down here. He recalls particularly his studies in the National Defence College which brought him in contact with many leading personalities and during which period he travelled to every nook and corner of the country. On account of his professional interest in Geophysics and Oceanography, he had many occasions to travel along the length and breadth of the Oceans and many continents. He is grateful to the Indian National Science Academy, New Delhi, Japanese Society for the Promotion of Science, the Czech Academy of Science, the Imperial Relations Trust, U.K. and the International Cultural Foundation of New York for making it possible for first hand experience and discussions in many countries including U.S.A., Japan, Czechoslovakia, U.K., etc.

2

FLUX IN INDIAN SOCIETY

1. Introduction

SOCIAL conditions and aspirations are never static and fixed. The changes are however sometimes slow and sometimes rapid. The conditions were ripe in India for rapid changes when the British consolidated their power by 1835 A.D. On account of imperial policy however, certain essentially desirable changes were deliberately sought to be slowed down. The official policy ever leaned backward in favour of reaction and obscurantism. Still the mind and experience of the East and the West had come in contact and the interaction led to brilliant flowering. Bankim Chander Chatterjee, Tagore, Prem Chand, Sayyed Ahmed, Raja Ram Mohan Roy, Swami Dayanand, Vivekanand, Sarojini Naidu, Tilak, Gokhale, Narain Guru, Iqbal, Gandhi, Nehru, Azad and many other great patriots, reformers and revolutionaries, strode over the length and breadth of the country. Indian society reflected the world at large, being an amalgam of many cultures developed within or outside the country. Indian environment was always assimilative.

Indians were great travellers both within and outside the country. Indian traders had set up agents along the entire coast of the land mass of Afro-Asia, and Indian emigrants and teachers had influenced entire continent of Asia as well as the island empires of South East Asia. Reciprocally they were not insular and welcomed people from outside in their midst. The Greeks, Tibetans, Huns, Iranians, Arabs, Turks, Thais and others that came to India in peace or as aggressors soon settled down as Indians. The Indian society had an ecological niche for every human way of life and for every calling. Ancient Jews, Christians and Parsis, all had welcome and good-will from the native population. Various caste and religious groups had symbiotic coexistence. The social set-up was accepted as an ordained society with the sanction of hoary usage. The inequalities were dismissed as rewards and punishments for one's deeds in this or earlier lives. The most respectable life of a religious aspirant was usually open to all howsoever lowly may their station be in ordinary life. Islam or christianity in India did not quarrel with the power structure in Indian society and joined the aristocracy or the professions for which they were fit. All Muslims could worship together while among the Hindus collective group worship was less common excepting in festivals and at pilgrim centres. As a direct response to new concepts of worship, a Bhakti movement of adoration of the deity and casteless religious movements developed on the Indian scene like the followers of Kabir and the Sikh Gurus.

On the economic plane the scene was static with little innovation and advancement of technology. The agriculture remained traditional. Handicrafts were well established and had a flourishing export market. It was to get a share in the Indian commerce that led to first Arab and later Europeon penetration of the East. Literacy and education was limited to few. At the beginning of the twentieth century we find the society fragmented in social intercourse but uniformly immersed in dire poverty. It was a life of affluent ease for the few and degrading servitude for the many. There were whole castes which had only menial service as a career for no wages and only meagre tips at the whim of their superiors. As late as 1928, in a place like the Punjab where caste barriers were supposed to be minimal, if a Muslim class fellow were to accidentally touch the cooked food meant for a Hindu child, the Hindu child stayed hungary that day and rejected the food. By 1946 many Hindus and Muslims had common meals at each others' houses. Now in 1985, Inter-caste and inter-religious marriages are quite common but ealier these were almost beyond imagination.

Ritualistic inhibitions were usually relaxed somewhat during travel and the opportunity to break such inhibitions was extensive in travelling by train, where the seats had to be shared with other passengers to whichever community and caste they may belong. There were however separate waiting rooms for Europeans ; thus the British in a way supported the common practice in India of separatism. Even the smallest railway station catered separately for Hindu or Muslims, especially the drinking water from the same water tank was handed to passengers by separate Hindu or Muslim water carriers. After Independence all this has gone like the dodo. Large scale urbanization started and has become a flood. Urbanization and money-based economics also reduce the distance between people. Conscious efforts for the eradication of feelings of group superiority and inferiority started with the movements begun by the reformers like Dayanand, Narain Guru and many others active in the national movement of Gandhi and Nehru. Spectacular unity was achieved by Bose in his Indian National Army movement in South East Asia. Untouchability is now a criminal offence after independence. There is no doubt that changes towards equality have galloped in the cities. The changes however have yet to catch up in some remote villages and in tribal life where the exploiting classes are still powerful and the common people are not aware of their rights. It is such exploiters that are confronted by violent revolutionaries like the secessionists and Naxalites.

2. The British as change agents

The British already had their reformation, renaissance and industrial revolution. The feudal ties did not exist to any degree. They brought a deeper knowledge of science, engineering and commerce. Contact with the Europeans was a great eye-opener for India. Even the Sanskrit literature which lay hidden, was retrieved by western scholarship. The system of higher education set up by the British put a premium on knowledge of English which became the medium of instruction for higher learning. This brought the new educated classes in intimate contact with the western culture through the literature and arts, music and poetry. It elicited an echo from the rediscovered ancient philosophy of India which is highly humanistic and universal. The Eastern and Western thought and ideals combined to combat casteism and parochialism. In the beginning, any kind of apartheid repelled the British. It was much later that the empire builders started studied avoidance of social contacts with the Indian classes. The reformation of the Indian society once started, picked up its own momentum and what could not be achieved in millenia was accomplished in few decades before and after independence.

The British embarked on many resource surveys and services and trained many Indians to assist them and carry forward these tasks which were equally important to free India as to the empire. One could mention the Botanical, Zoological, Geographical and the Geological surveys, statistical organizations, meteorologica l services, railways, telegraph and the telephone services. They introduced many economic plants and plantations and carried through technological inputs into every sphere. They however did not interfere with common usage. The economic exploitation of Indians by Indians and of all Indians by the British continued.

In the pre-British days, official positions were auctioned so that the successful bidder could squeeze as much profit from the office as he possibly could. The British made a break with this practice, but the wages were invariably very low and customary exploitation of the public continued merrily. The exploiting potential of petty officials and money-lenders in fact increased since the Sahibs could be approached only through proper channel and through the written word by his underlings. The extra income through bribery became a standard perk for any lowly job. It is becoming increasingly difficult to rectify the situation. Honest and efficient work now enjoins society to raise the salaries quickly all around and then educate the public for expecting service without bribery. The straws in the wind are the extraordinary pay scales from usual Indian standards for the bank employees, armed forces and top officials of public sector on the one hand and revolts and strikes in certain services where either the emoluments are too low or the graft is not enough to percolate to all.

England-centered modern education began about a century ago. Knowledge of Indian languages, and culture has also been added on. The quality of education got diluted when considerable expansion of education as well as professional openings took place after independence. Universities and colleges were started, producing in fact bad copies of some prestigious Indian and foreign institutions. The goal of education became just to pass an examination somehow and not to acquire culture and discrimination. Even preparation for earning a livclihood was half-hearted.

The educated tended to become snobs and incompetent to stand on their own. There is already a reaction and many services and professions now prefer to train relatively younger recruits by apprenticeships or continuing education. For spread of higher education, correspondence courses and open universities are now coming up on the British models. Science education has expanded in bulk only after independence, though modern science education has a history of about a hundred years in the country.

3. Communalism and Gandhism

History books are totally silent about any communal clashes before the British rule. Most experts agree that the divide and rule tactics of the British led to communal bickerings after the upheavals of the mutiny of 1857 and the agitations after the first world war. Europeans had a background of bloody communal conflicts and the Indian history was also interpreted as the Muslim attack on Hindu India or the Hindu social tyranny on the poor Muslims or Hindu rebellion against the glorious Islamic state. The territorial aggrendisement was taken as the struggle of Hindus and Muslims. The nature of communal riots in India is such that they must be ascribed to an hidden hand of certain vested interests and to manipulation. Excepting the semi-political communal riots in the wake of partition, the riots rarely touched the villages. Realizing that the poison of communalism was not getting under control, the Indian leaders agreed to the partition of the country into two independent sovereign secular states, one with a Muslim majority and one with a Hindu majority. The Indian state stayed secular while Pakistan soon declared itself to be an Islamic State with somewhat less rights for non-Muslims and soon they started giving fine and exclusive definition of Muslims. The break-away Bangladesh from larger Pakistan is still not fully decided whether to develop her secularism or not.

Secularism, that is equal respect for all religions and that holds economic and political rights to be independent of religious labels, is essential for a multicommunal, multi-lingual nation. Still our secularism is not yet thoroughly entrenched and the integration of the Indian polity into a single nation is still not complete. Doubtful leaders of certain misguided insecure groups have become adepts in raising communal passions and riding on such hysteria to communal or political importance. The most recent communal disruption of Khalistanis in the affairs of the country and the dastardly murder of prime minister Indira Gandhi and its aftermath has jolted the entire people into a realization of the frail nature yet of the communal integration in the country that it can be violated with almost impunity by a bunch of determined terrorists or interansingent pseudo-leaders depending to some extent on foreign based means and propaganda. The nation has reacted sharply and besides being liberal to all patriotic groups is out to suppress crimes against national unity. One expects that modern means of mass communication and objective acceptance of legitimate goals of all will be skillfully used for integration and intercommunal amity.

In modern society, the interpersonal relations of dependence and cooperation are giving way to competition and exploitative market relationships. The concept of contented thankfulness is giving way to acquisitive ethics. If we continue on the path of unalloyed capitalism in the ever expanding private sector, and the motives of private profit remain paramount, it will become correspondingly difficult to pursue the equally important goals of social justice and acceptable social impact of development. The classical remedy of piety has already failed. The Marxist-Leninist remedies have flopped in China. The remedy very likely lies in Gandhism which is pragmatic and harnesses machines as well as handicrafts, science as well as vocational education, defines God as truth and harps on service of the masses and the trusteeship of the affluent along with socialism of sorts. Family ties are breaking up ever since the cities became easily accessible due to fast means of communication. The ties of village and family have loosened. Large joint families provided both stability as well as security against scarcity. These were useful for the economics of scarcity and not for actual or potential abundance. Now-a-days when each adolescent desires for a scooter and a transistor, the self-denying ethos of joint family or even a commune has no furture. In the prevailing climate of self-interest and superficial politeness, Gandhian accent on sincerity, simplicity and truth will provide much needed corrective.

4. Cultural aspects

Religion in India has had an important place for rituals, fasts, fairs and festivals. Whatever now exists is often commercialised as attractions for tourists and funseekers. There is distance between centres of science and industry and festivals around religious fervor. People have become leisure and entertainment minded and the entertainment is more often passive provided by bouts in stadia, radio or television. In mature India of the future participative cultural activities must again become important. Social pressure has to develope for this.

There have been revolutionary changes in marriage customs. The distant western scheme of love marriages and films have had great impact on the youth. But the youth is gripped by double thinking. Often he wants to select a girl through love and also get a considerable dowry and in addition a control of wife's share of her father's property as soon as possible. The girl's parents have opposite ideas. Self-arranged marriages are on the increase now compared to love/trial marriages even in USA. This gives them wider choice and objective appreciation of the possible alternatives. Full share of daughter in her parents property, though a welcome blow for women rights has led to many complications. In a preponderingly agricultural community, it is difficult to alienate a portion of real estate to a different family often resident of a different place. Very often daughters are prevailed upon to forswear the parental inheritence or in the absence of any proper will, litigation ensues between close relations. One of the complaints of Akali agitation in the Punjab was around this step of conferring property rights on the daughters. The problem of dowry has become acute inspite of government rules regarding primary right of the bride on all dowry and wedding gifts. Women must have equal property rights, but certain steps can be taken to remove the difficulties for happy married life of the daughter in her husband's family. By custom all marriages should be solemnised in government registry. The father's property could be evaluated and daughter' share announced so that everyone is clear about the expected rupee equivalent at one go or in mutually acceptable instalments. This will do away with dowry as well as future litigation and any accretion in future to respective properties will not be subject of controversy. Any subsequent exchange of gifts between brot hers and sisters will depend only on their pleasure and mutual affection. The legal possibility of divorce is also a step towards better marital relations.

India is very rich in natural beauty. The climate in most parts is mild. People are fond of walks, pilgrimages, health discipline. For the youth however, late mornings are more fashionable since they prefer late evening entertainment provided by TV and other media. There are however incentives in the form of activities of national youth and sports organizations and new adventure societies. There are many organization encouraging adventurous exploration of mountains, rivers and oceans.

Any society may be judged by the position of women. The women had an honoured place in the Aryan society. The position deteriorated in the past few centuries due to foreign invasions and internal unrest. There was decadence in court life and absence of leisured classes in Hindu society. Only the reformers during the British period e.g. Swami Dayanand who established the Arya Samaj worked for the uplift and education of women. Participation along with the men-folk by the women in the national liberation struggle brought about equality of women with the men-folk. Recent legal provision for divorce and inheritence by daughters have given them great relief. In view of the great deal of crime and cruelty against women, society has to take stringent steps to safeguard the position and honour of women.

5. Conclusion

If one were to go by our roots, the natural development of the Indian society would be like that of Japan. Like the Japanese our industrial labour would also have loyalty to the capitalist owners regarding them as roughly family elders. Indian traders and bankers were world famous for their business ethics and fulfilling their promises. Indian history is full of incidents bringing out patriotism and sacrifice. But evolution has carried out here a different experiment than in Japan. To a background similar to that of Japan, there has been a centuries old interaction with the central Asian tribes and the West. The result therefore must approach the average culture of the whole world. Let us hope that best of all streams of culture survive and are strengthened by our own genius. An educational effort will be necessary at the level of a crusade for reminding our young men of the ancient virtues of sacrifice, simplicity and idealism that have invariably produced great Indians who shine in the pages of a glorious history.

3

PRE-INDEPENDENCE SOCIETY

1. Introduction

During the war days, the conditions were abnormal. Inflation and shortages had set in. Indian war-time contractors were making money. The nation was sullen and the only enthusiasm was shown by the minuscule communist party in favour of the war effort since it also helped the Soviet Union. Volunteers were thronging to join the British Indian Army from a mixture of motives and the Indian soldiers from the Japanese prisoners of war camps were volunteering for the Indian National Army from patriotic motives. Those were the days of the catastrophic man-made Bengal famine. For analysis of the pre-independence society we shall be looking primarily at the days intervening the two world wars. The country was impoverished to the extreme. Handicrafts had hardly any internal or external market in competetion with the flood of cheap European or Japanese industrial goods. Agriculture was primitive. Soil, forests and animal wealth had been impoverished. The population was static or growing negligibly mainly because of the high mortality among children. Houses and streets in most villages and small towns were dilapidated and people were staying in ruins, or mud hovels. The agriculture could support the population at subsistance level. No starvation was visible. Even though the state hardly worried about the development of the land in any effective manner, but in place of welfare state, the society had the insurance of joint family for everybody's food and shelter. The colonial regime was a business-like affair balancing its books for internal and external security and the minimum expenditure neccssary for the containued exploitaion and maintenance of the country as a happy hunting ground for Europeans and their loyal princes and servants.

Villages had become slums of the worst kind. Elementary hygiene was missing and even now there is not much to boast of in the matter of village or even city hygiene. People were most of the time idle except when engaged on unavoidable agricultural chores. They were hungry for news of the wide world and the statements of communal and national leaders. Women had continuous drudgery as their fate whether in the slums or big houses of the cities. Scavenging work was routine though the scavengers who were the unfortunate untouchables and had no clue or incentive for cleanliness. Even the fixing of long conveient handles to the brooms wielded by the untouchable awaited independence for that simple innovation, since the common man had no concept of the difficulty of the scavengers. The streets in towns were lit by kerosene lamps on dark nights only. Some industries, large towns and a lucky rich man had electricity from the town supply or from a captive imported generator.

The dilapidation and deterioration of dwellings were clear indication that the people lived from hand to mouth and they must have had superior standards about a century earlier when they constructed the dwellings in the first place. They had neither the reasources nor personal skills to maintain the once elegant structures that now grinned at them. Many old residents had almost no visible income unless the produce of couple of inherited trees or a cow be regarded as their sole riches. A whole lot of people were engaged in infinitesimal trade. The meagre goods changed many hands before reaching the poor consumer, unless he tendent to depend on his own home-made grains and goods. Prices were low and cash was scarce. The current inflation and high prices of grains has boosted the standards of the common man, even through this may be against ordinary calculations. When they did not know any better, most people were contented with their lot. Lower caste people were readily available for traditional tasks for practically no wages. Regular castes were available for the traditional tasks or religious rituals, provision of music and entertainment at family celebrations, fetching water from community wells or tanks, match making, personal haircuts etc. etc. The children of most Brahmins and lower castes stuck to traditional professions and filial apprenticeships. Only the children of shopkeepers and money lenders sought new education. Educated unemployment had begun to plague the country and many educated persons were partly available for the political movements including joining the army for the victory of the allies.

The education was accessible to only the well-to-do or to outstanding youngsters. Executive jobs or almost any jobs were open only to nominees of influential people. This legacy we have yet to overcome. The society in this period was in general still stratified. Castes governed day to day work for most people. Life was extremely comfortable for the lucky few with adequate means of livelihood, and with suitable higher caste label. Under the British Indian law, the money-lenders and traders flourished and started thinking of fresh manufactures and supported political movements for cornering the internal market and recapturing some share of the export markets of old. Wage slavery, bond slavery, practically sale of women and children were rampant. Disease or beggary was a common sight. Begging had hoary sanction and prestige, counting on the charity and hospitality ingrained among Indians of all faiths and fortunes. There was no institutional handling of the Indian systems of therapy that were in the hands of isolated and uneducated practitioners and the modern medicine could hardly cater even to civil and military government servants.

India had a large population and the details of the social system often differred in different regions e.g. those growing wheat or rice or living in mountainous regions or coastal and desert regions. The economy and life of regions growing cash crops like tea, copra or tobacco were again different. Mixing of castes and communities had continued in schools but any loosening of the caste hold was not very much in evidence except in the wake of the politico-religious movements.

2. The decay in Indian society

The roots of the Indian society are in the Vedic philosophy. The ideal society was of righteousness, fair play and performance of enjoined rituals. The masses were well prepared for their intellectual needs by the mass inculcation of the art of living and social behaviour through the intensive folk learning of Ramayana and the Mahabharata as well as the myths and legends available from the rich heritage contributed by the literature and the teachings of Buddhists, Jains, and Muslims and many other races and tribes that lived in the land. Indian businessmen enjoyed from ancient times the reputation of good businees dealings and frugality coupled with hard work. In the Vedic period women had same rights as men, though great majority must have shared the same jobs as men. A married couple was considered as a single unit for all practical purposes. Many women were highly educated and were engaged in teaching or philosophical controversies. The society in ancient India was similar to that of ancient Greece or Rome with the difference that there was no slavery though professions in general passed on from father to son.

There was however a period of decay and dark ages set in particularly for Hindu thought due to internecine warfare and inconclusive empire building efforts for long periods punctuated by short spells of stability. In the troubled times royal patronage to Hindu learning became negligible. The ancient texts were almost lost. Women became objects of loot or slaves for security, ever worshipping their husbands and masters. Foreign idiom and vernaculars prevailed, the rich ancient texts became un-understandable. Ancient beliefs became rituals. The professional castes became castes by birth. Untouchability provided all the cheap labour to higher castes. Most temples were inaccessible to untouchables. Widows were debarred from remarriage. All kinds of beggars roamed the country-side cashing on the blind faith of the masses. The lofty principles of religion and philosophy were enslaved to the greed of ignorant people. Miracles abounded. The genuine article was submerged in a plethora of magical signs for the gullible. Only a few embarked on the narrow uphill road of competitive success in education or technical work or perhaps on the still harder path of renunciation and self-realization. In general there was a stagnation like the one before the French revolution. However the regeneration of society had already started at various centres around individual zealots : religious reformists or stormy rebels.

Charity has been extolled in the Indian culture and both Hindus and Muslims regard being charitable as the core quality of a religious individual. But there has hardly ever been a community charity movement of all citizens of a town as happens so often in the United States. Only some sectarian charity was visible as collected and distributed by the Bohras, Arya Samaj,

Radha-Saomis etc or certain popular godmen. Common people felt charitable by leaving few morsals for the beggars and birds or occasionally throwing some small coins to beggars or to the attendant at a wayside shrine or at the tomb of a recluse. Still the charitable urge cultivated by centuries of exhortation would occasionally produce stalwarts like Ganga Ram or Alagappa* to shower their environment with charitable institutions like schools, temples, hospitals and orphanages.

3. The re-awakening

The struggle for social transiormation and national independence was irrevocably developing. Thanks to the leadership which was far ahead of their times, the struggle practically followed a peaceful course. Mahatma Gandhi practically enunciated the philosophy that society can be improved only by non-violence though it may be defended even by violence if the losses otherwise would be unbearable. It was this enlightened leadership that granted adult franchise, equal rights for women and equality before law, freedom of press etc before the affected masses even were fully conscious of the disabilities they had been suffering from.

Society is primarily inter-personal and intergroup relationships. In this context the pre-independence society was almost utopian. The obedience to the head of the family, respect for age, and group coddling of children was universal. Looked at from the modern day high ground, the housewife was worked to disease and premature old age, but she was the embodiment of sacrifice and devotion. People were relatively more honest. Recreation was in many ways participative, like folk songs, folk dancing, play acting, story telling, and entertainment by professional castes of actors and jokers. Talking films became however very popular from their beginning in 1930 and makeshift cinema halls spread to the countryside. Now-a-days most entertainment is passive from the radio, TV and films.

Most British civilian officers were respected for their

* Ganga Ram, Sir, was an engineer and agriculturist of repute and a philanthropist of the Punjab. He proceeded in building and innovating many irrigation schemes. Alagappa Chettiar was a famous philanthropist and educationist of Tamil Nadu. He had business interests far and wide.

integrity, sense of fair play, and some of them were very much involved in reconstruction work despite the bureaucratic constraints. The rich especially the titled gentry or the feudal aristocracy emulated the British in the pastimes of sports, hunts, golf, clubbing and frequenting of hill resorts in summer heat.

The people came to credit the Europeans with superior scientific and technical knowledge. Even the teachers of elementary science were Europeans or followed British text books. The technical services and surveys were mostly officered by the British. Under their tutelage, archeology, museums and archives were set up and certain princely states also adorned their capital cities with such collections. Some gifted Indians became prominent in science and technology in this period. The combined efforts of European savants and some sympathetic administrators and many enlightened Indians pulled India out of slumber.

4. Conflicts and agitations

At the beginning of the interwar period, there was unity in the demand for political rights. During this period the strategy of divide and rule was intensified and communalism received encouragement from the rulers which has since not been fully overcome inspite of the partition of the country. The poison of communalism was introduced rather in a subtle manner chiefly through communal misrepresentation in history texts and in giving communal twist to economic factors as experienced by people and often expressed in folklore. The new authoritative pronouncements in different contexts emphasized disparagement of different communities : The khatris are Jews, the Sikhs are unwise, the Muslims are improvident, the Jats are ambitious, the Chinese are spineless, the Pathans are wild etc., etc. History was presented as communal aggressions and rebellions. Civic responsibility became secondary to insistence on communal rights even when these clashed with those of the other communities. In cities, where Hindus and Muslims often lived next to each other, new segregated localities started growing. The diversity was so much accented, that even linguistic unity was threatened among different communities. Petty quarrels often took a communal turn in cities were agents provocateurs could function, and each year communal disturbances occurred in some towns. The communalism and miscalculations of communal forces led to the partition riots. Some major problems of free India still stem from similar communalism, linguism and regionalism. The theoretical notions of class war were sought to be applied to communities and castes. Thus modern prejudices were pasted on older irrational concepts. Freedom struggle sharpened the tools of mass protest like strikes, peaceful movements against certain chosen laws, no tax campaigns, processions, public meetings for expressing disaffection etc. etc. Social and commercial boycotts were often pressed. Even when there is now a democratic responsible sovereign government, the agitational approach of the disaffected groups persists. Resort to non-violent and sometimes violent agitations by the students, youth, low paid employees or even the police personnel for redress of their grievances is a legacy of the struggle for freedom and reflects poorly on the new managers and intellectual resources of the country. A democratic government must attempt to forestall disaffection especially among its employees and most groups in a free country must give due regard to national interest. India is pursuing a socialist pattern of society and welfare of the common man is the avowed national policy. The welfare activities including free education and assistance by loans for self-employment, grants against calamities of all kinds are now regular charge on government or semi-government funds. But during the communal hey-dey certain fanatic elements got entrenched in the control of certain religious charities and endowments. Such elements have a vested interest in communal or regional agitations and they can also draw on financial and terroristic resources from abroad among agents of foreign states not well disposed to India or among expatriates from the times of the spreading of the communal poison in India. In free India some national supervision of endowments and charities restricted to particular groups has to be ensured perhaps by new acts of parliament. In secular India charity too must not create divisons. Often foreign believers pour in money for the upkeep of sectional preachers and religious places. All such remittances should be decentralised only from a national pool so that deserving poor of all denominations get assistance, meeting also as far as possible the wishes of the donors by adding funds from local resources.

5, Leisure, health and environment

During the period under discussion, televisions had not been invented or introduced, radio had become an acquisition of the wealthy. During the world war, people collected near radio sets for news broadcasts. The tradition of drama and folk plays existed. Apart from religious renderings, plays with revolutionary fervour were often staged under the garb of historical or social stories. Leisure was universal but interpersonal interest of everyone did not allow people to become listless as one observes in the poverty stricken unemployed in the slums of the west. Religious observances and festivals were plentiful to keep everyone on his toes. There was considerable merit in listening to mythological renderings by artists who could often quote or sing in illustration of their story. Company of holy men and mendicants was also considered a meritorious action. There is much more use of drinking and intoxicants now than it was in this period. Child births, marriages were long drawn out affairs involving celebration by the affected people and their neighbours. Every mourning demanded a helping hand in mournful chants, and long respectful sittings honouring the dead and consoling the bereaved ones.

In India noise and company is usually welcome. The day begins with singing of the birds and chanting of hymns almost in every household and neighbourhood shrine. Indian caste system had invented hereditary musicians, dancers and entertainers. They provided entertainment and class to people for a pittance. Sometimes even the caste system pointed out to certain influential families their caste duty to arrange such entertainment. It was interesting to find the professionals doing their duty when the audience was missing since they enjoyed gaining merit by singing or dancing as their duty when once asked to perform. In India there are two distinct types of singing. In Karnataka music the tones are slightly different. It is possible that at one time in the hoary past, the Karnataka music also began in the north. The professional caste of house-hold singers in the Punjab prefer to sing in Karnataka style. Folk entertainers often visited neighbouring villages on their own. People had always been fond of cultural entertainment and the style was not blunted by poverty. Many times individuals refused to work throughout the year if they could make enough in few months to spend the remainder period in trekking on a pilgrimage. Travel and touring as a pilgrim was quite economical. The climate was mild and temples etc had cheap or often free guest accommodation.

The common man enjoyed his leisure. The wayside pools provided fishing. Taming and training of birds, parrots and nightingales or partridges was very much in vogue. Hunts were popular. Only when the deer and many other species were decimated after independence, people have realized the necessity of conservation and bird watching and photography of wild animals in national reserves have become sportsmanlike. Bullock cart racing, cock fighting etc. were gambling sport. Every locality boasted of a simple wrestling arena. Children had innumerable outdoor games requiring hardly much apparatus.

The colonial history books call Indians as a stay-at-home people which is rather misleading. Indian armies during the British rule fought in almost all continents for the preservation of the Empire. It was lucky for the United States that they won their freedom rather early as otherwise the British Indian army might have kept them safe for the commonwealth. Indians have always been moving out to colonise or for earning a livelihood. During recent times they opened up Africa for internal commerce. Indian plantation workers and settlers have recently spread to Malayasia, Sri Lanka, Mauritius, Trinidad etc. The oil rich countries of the Arab world have now attracted a great many Indians among others. India has a long history of peaceful settlements abroad. Even the ancient Phoenicians have tentatively been identified with South Indian sailors. Indians though mostly plains people thought nothing of spending their old age in Himalayan retreats. Their adventurous journeys often led them across the Tibetan plateau to central Asia, Korea and Japan. It is true that the spirit of adventure was dormant for some time for lack of patronage. In free India it is quite evident in their exploration of India's rivers and seas or in the exploration of Antarctica and also the Himalayas. A people who honour vagabonds and recluses, who accept renunciation as a normal occurrence, whose national dress is the undress and for whom fasting and simple living is virtuous, will naturally be adventurous. The Indian character is evident from their development of yoga an adjunct to mental and physical fitness which is highly peace oriented and has spiritual overtones.

The life expectency at birth was very low mainly because of child mortality since the connection between hygience and prevention of disease was not known. There were many diseases in the tropical country for which proper treatment did not exist. The Indian system of medicine was almost like the Greek system which itself was available almost in its ancient way. The materia medica was richer than the same of any other country. The life expetancy was much higher for a five year old. Ravages of malaria, TB and many fell diseases have been eliminated only by modern medicine after independence. Old people were very well looked after, though these would not be very many. Magic cures were resorted to for many diseases that had no medicinal cures. Superstition, trust in black magic and evil eye was common. In one part of the country children were branded so that they escape the evil eye. People took their mental worries to gurus and godmen for alleviation. They were the psychiatrist equivalents just as they flourish even now. Often faith really cured the pious. Inspite of individual ritual bathing and cleanliness there was no concept of civic sense or of hygiene. It was rare (and still is) to see an efficient municipal committee attending to removal of sewage and garbage. Complacency has led to the pollution of the holy Ganges whose waters were supposed to have germicidal purifying powers.

Indians had and still have fraternal feelings for plants and animals. Even the invocation for peace specifically mentions peace for the vegetation and animal kingdom. As a part of grace before meals, a morsel or two were kept separately for the birds or animals. It was considered sinful to lop branches of a shade giving tree. Though ancient Harappan cities boasted of underground sewage, most villages and towns did not have any civic services. This must have happened because of the free services of the untouchables for menial manual work. Since the better classes would not attend at all, the tools of trade for cleaning and hygiene remained primitive. The result of this colossal neglect is still visible. New suburbs are growing without elementary facilities. Sweepers are also not readily available because all the other professions are readily open to them and other castes have not yet taken to the conservancy services even though these should be now lucrative.

6. Communications and production

Communications were well advanced. Railway system was the largest passenger carrying system in the world. The facilities were minimal but the fares were also extremely low. Most of the goods traffic was either by rail or by bullock carts. Post and telegraphic links were covering the entire country. Only large cities boasted of telephones. Dakota flights operated during the war years between major towns. Radar was not known, radio communication was established. People were prone to consult astrologers for future events and festival periods. People believed in supernatural powers of certain holy men or holy artefacts. Belief in extra-sensory perception was common, and adepts claimed to a capacity to point out thiefs or underground sources of water like wells buried long ago.

Freedom of speech and association was frowned upon, but the people exercised these inspite of repression. The press was fearless and had an important role in the freedom struggle. Many Indians served the empire, but many more waged the non-violent opposition. Mass rallies were common-place. Mahatma Gandhi had novel ways to touch the hearts of people. Symbols and slogans were used with great dexterity to rouse the people. Reliance on truth and sincerity proved mightier than any propaganda or greed.

British consolidation had resulted in the destruction of cottage industries and handicrafts which were the major standby activities of the agricultural population. Agriculture was further impoverished in the absence of any inputs because of innocence of advanced knowledge or better cattle or instruments. Industrial goods of all kinds had been imported mainly from England. The logic of supplies and war preparations, continuous agitation for better deal for the poor in villages and certain progress in responsible government made it possible for government support in the growth of agricultural sciences, animal husbandry and engineering. Parsi and Marwari entrepreuners started industrial enterprises. Nehru set up his non-official planning department in the congress organization. There were many campaigns for the use of Indian made (swadeshi) products. Village industries and handloom organizations were intensely supported by the politically awakened masses.

The savings of the rulers went into capital formation in U.K.

British invesments in India were often in large services like railways where considerable infra-structure was paid for by the British Indian government or in plantations and production of cash crops for export. The income which must have been fabulous of most of the Indian princes went in idle display and was squandered in the resorts of Europe. Their capital towns boasted of toy trains, pleasure palaces and gardens and wine and women fests.

The maintenance of means of communication like the railways and telegraphs ushered in technical awareness of many Indian employees, and the common people. The national movement rediscovered the handicrafts and also helped the budding Indian textile and other industries to get established. Industrialization and wide economic activity got a big boost on account of the war effort in India. On account of Indian war time supplies and services India became a creditor country at the end of the war which also contributed to her quick deliverence from bondage after the war.

4

GRAFTING OF MODERN SCIENCE IN INDIA

1. Introduction

Grafting of plants can be carried out only in kindred species. The sap of the stock has to reach the scion. Grafting of modern science was possible because Indian mind also had the same initial pattern as that of the Greek mind. The two had direct interaction in ancient times. The scientific advancement in England also correlated with the establishment of British sway over India. The revolutionary and reformist movements and spread of democratic opportunities for learning for all some-how assisted in the advancement of modern science in Europe. India also was ripe for reforms and caste restrictions on learning were being removed. The science based western civilization regards itself as the direct descendent of Greek thought which lay eclipsed on account of the sway of dogma and acceptance of slavery.

Science was the outcome of maturity of reasoning mind which began seeking answers to questions, and verifying the same. The whole process was open to anyone's scrutiny or repetition. Dogmatic acceptance of authority was frowned upon. The questions asked were for the sake of knowledge and not from the usual religious motives of personal salvation. When the British power was consolidated in India in 1857, they already had machine based industry in their country for well night two centuries. The grafting of science and technology in India was carried out leisurely. The new apprentices were selected from a vast population and had to have initiative and aspirations. It was often noted that the Indians were keen enquirers and prone to scientific temper, given the opportunity. It was the inevitable result of relative apathy born of caste assurances, that any indigenous scientific insights or the method of experimental verification did not begin here as in Europe of the pre-modern times.

2. The Indian mind

While the Greek civilization penetrated Europe in a round about manner through the Arab centres of learning in Sicily and Spain acting as intermediaries, the Greeks had directly interacted with Indian culture. The philosophy, science and technology of the two contemporary civilizations were very much in touch with each other and had liberally exchanged ideas. Hinduised Greek states persisted in the north west corner of India as well as in the neighbourhood of India for about half a millennium. India had the ability to forestall most of Greek philosophy and go beyond as in the invention of the zero. They also had speculated on the atomic theory and in addition proclaimed the objective reality of consciousness, a highly modern concept. Speculative controversy and argumentative philosophy was quite common. Just as the Greek thought experienced a bloc due to the practice of slavery, Indian practical side was blocked by the institution of almost free slavery through the practice of untouchability. Use of machines can advance only if labour costs are high or the need of large scale production exists through enriched or captive markets. In India the needs could be met by wide-spread handicraft skills. In fact there was considerable surplus for export. The crafts were held in families and passed on from parents to off-spring. In such a situation even simple advancement in traditional tools was considered a sacrilege and not necessary. Time and skills were abundant and such manufactured articles were pieces of art. Indian wares were prized all over the world and most trade was in favour of India which was a rich country having gathered the precious metals from all over the world for her manufactured artifacts. The riches can even now be imagined from the usual practice of every builder placing a piece of gold or silver when fixing the first brick in the foundation of his dwelling.

Peculiarly, the Indian religions had no place for the devil or any original sin. Though the straight and narrow path of piety and righteousness was respected, the ordinary religious duties of an individual included earning of wealth and the fulfilment of wordly desires. Aiming at salvation through the performance of religious and social duties only followed in priority the wordly exhortations. Life was divided into stage of learning, earning and duties of a house-holder, social service and freedom from ownership. Thus there was a respectable place for work, fun, service as well as meditation. The intellectuals loved to spin words than worry about better tools for the artisans. The spirit of enquiry was very much there but the direction it took was of other-worldly speculation and not for better understanding of nature or mastery over resources. Whatever one learned about matter was empirical, laboriously gleaned by observation or at the feet of preceptors and was guarded as a source of power over the uninformed multitude. The empirical knowledge was not analysed to produce insights or theories for further guesses and successes.

The only tools the Hindus had invented from their preoccupation with spiritual quantum jumps were magical diagrams and spells. The simple chemicals and special materials were shrouded with mystery as dangerous knowledge fit to be used only by religious leaders for working miracles. From ancient times however close relationship of love and respect had been developed for teachers. Many young men quickly flocked to great science teachers like Saha, Raman, Kothari, Bose and Kichlu and chose to pursue scientific vocation. The system has however been grossly diluted later on account of teachers of lower calibre (since other professions offerred better rewards to scientists) and indifferent students since the accent came to be placed only on the acquisition of degrees (which could be had by the favour of the teacher who also began to have a vested interest in the expansion of the list of his successful students) and not in the acquisition of knowledge and expertise in the subject itself. The present system is devalued because both the teachers and the taught are not objectively selected but happen to be around on account of wrong policies and prejudices. There is authorised illogical admission procedure and dimming of the value system. A better system should be liberal stipends based on the consideration of means of students and liberal pre-admission coaching of aspiring students without in any way lowering of standards for admission for any one, either persons from influential families or from politically supported classes. There must not be lowering of standards for any one at the time of first entry into a service or at promotion points. Again there can be free extra coaching for candidates from backward classes before selection purely by merit in competition with others. Such steps have been fruitfully adopted in selection of military officers. The favours to castes and religious groups had started during the British period and has insidiously expanded later. Better way would be to bring up in couple of generations the backward class children by special schooling and intensive socially supported coaching.

The horizons before the Indian mind were limitless from their catholic and secular outlook. The philosophical insistence on truth and performance prepared them for accepting new ideas and checking if these worked. Even the Vedas had enjoined "Let noble thoughts come to us from all sides". For India science was an important aspect of truth and knowledge to be mastered. There was no conflict of their theological beliefs with science. By a peculiar dichotomy, India could always let belief and unbelief coexist in different compartments like the different states of an elementary particle.

The Indians had an holistic approach to environment. They never imagined the whole creation to be centered around man and exist only for his benefit. They experienced kinship with animals and birds. The wide-spread neglect and pollution of the environment is primarily due to ignorance of proper husbandry and dire survival needs, but it has happened inspite of their reverence for the environment and one is hopeful that now after the proven extravagent misuse of nature they will master the science of environmental upkeep. Many constructive decisions are now everyday occurrence like the preservation of the Silent Valley in the south and giant schemes for the preservation of the Himalayan ecosystem and plans for the revival of the purity of Ganga river flow.

The hold of tradition, blind obedience to elders, subsistence economy, addiction to decadent luxury, were the prime causes of neglect of innovation. The aristocracy who had the leisure to support education and teachers had no hand in the work of production : agricultural or industrial. They had their assured position and wealth from the exploitation of the poor and the untouchables. The intellectual effort was spent in the barren work of commenting on the ancient obscure texts, or compiling tantric mythology. Even before the arrival of the British, some communication existed with the outer world of knowledge through visits of renowned Muslim scholars but their influence was more in their carrying away translations of mutual works or increasing the influence of different schools of Islamic theology and handing over some current knowledge of Arab astronomy and medicine. But the source of enquiry was itself drying up in Islamic lands and they have yet to recover from periodic onslaughts of fanaticism for some kind of authority or the other. India did acquire from them new military logistics and mutual synergistic growth of song and dance, sports and fun, chivalry and tournaments. Magnificent secular and religious structures and monuments were built reflecting highest international building skills or techniques in sculpture and engraving arts. The land was dotted with irrigation tanks though often in disrepair on account of long periods of anarchy. The spirit of hospitality was however always strong.

3. Science, the talisman for prosperity

The symbol of modern technology in India was not electrification or chemical fertilizers, but it was the steam engine. The railways that were built in the mid-nineteenth century brought home to the people the new science and technology which the Europeans possessed. The people who were recruited and trained to operate and maintain the railway system were the first Indian technicians. Signals and telegraph were naturally developed along with the railways and this meant the introduction of electrical communication. On the other hand the grafting of production technology was delayed in the fond hope that India could stay a captive market for everything from a pin to a railway engine for the European industries. The reluctant industrialization was however enforced by circumstances pertaining to the two world wars. A genuine transfer of resources and technology however took place only after India's independence when due to cold war the USSR sought and won friendship with India for mutual benefit. The grafting has become a flood on account of the emulation by the west in aiding industrial production in countries like India to save these even partially for capitalism and free enterprise. India is now said to have crossed the take-off stage and can participate on her own in the production of new technologies and is already exporting all kinds of products and technical experience to friendly foreign countries.

The initial introduction of science in India is the story of dedicated and highly motivated European scientists who came to India to duplicate the scientific investigations and institutions which had been set up in England, Some of the well known names are John Gerhard Koenig (1728-1781), the natural historian of the East India Company, William Roxburgh and his English successors as honorary superintendents of the Royal Botanical Gardens at Calcutta. Among the successors was one George King who began the publication of the Annals of the Royal Botanical Garden and also set up the Botanical Survey of India (1890). The Botanical Survey was instrumental in establishing many commercially important crops into India, like tea, rubber, coffee, potato, cinchona, tobacco etc. Many British botanists compiled famous treatises on Indian regional or other types of flora. Many famous Indian botanists have continued such work with credit. E. Blyth published in 1852 his catalogue of Indian birds. Melleland produced the classic 'Fishes of India' (1878). The Zoological Survey of India was set up in 1916. Famous Indian zoologists include S.L. Hora and Salim Ali. James Rennell, the Surveyor General produced the first map of Hindustan (1783). William Lambton (1753-1823) started the great trignometric survey of India. George Everest was also a surveyor general in whose honour Mount Everest was named by Andrew Waugh. Famous Indian surveyors who worked on surveys were Radhanath Sikdar and Mohim Husain.

Geology naturally received considerable attention because of the natural curiosity of the state in the mineral wealth of the country and in order to assist dam building and various irrigation projects. The geology of the Himalayas began to be studied in 1831. Hugh Falconer explored the geological formation of the Siwalik Hills. D.H. Williams of the British Geological Survey laid the foundation of the Geological Survey of India (1851). Thomas Oldham expanded the Geological Survey and trained Indians in basic scientific work connected with surveying. From among the geologists trained by him was P.N. Bose who was very much a factor in drawing the attention of J.N. Tata to the deposits of rich iron ore and coking coal of India. J.H. Pratt propounded his isostasy haypothesis from his gravity surveys in India.

H. Piddington studied cyclones and set up cyclone warning service at Calcutta from the Alipore observatory from 1865. H.F. Blanford was the first Meteorological Reporter to the Government of India when the Meteorological Department was set up in 1875. By 1878 there were 128 meteorological observatories. Even as late as 1939, the only openings available to physicists in India besides the teaching profession were in the Metorological Department or the fledgeling All India Radio. Systematic knowlege of weather and climate of India is in the works of Blanford and Eliot. H.H Field pioneered the use of upper air data for weather forecasting. Indian made meteorological instruments were exported to many foreigin observatories. In 1893 a solar physics observatory was set up at Kodaikanal with M. Smith as the superintendent. Ths Madras observatory had been functioning informally since 1787 with many noted astronomers contributing for their star atlases and making original observations on asteroids and variable stars. In 1909 Evershed studied solar prominences at the Kodaikanal observatory and discovered the radial motion of sunspots. The Alibag Magnetic Observatory established originally in 1840 at Colaba (Bombay) is regarded as a primary observatory. William Jones was the founder president of the Asiatic Society which nurtured and stimulated the intellectual activity in the arts and the sciences. In 1832 the society started the scientific journal of the Asiatic Society and in 1814, the oriental museum of the society was set up with Nathaniel Wallich as honorary superintendent. The Archelogical Survey with Alexander Cunningham as the surveyor General was set up in 1867. John Marshall was appointed in 1902 as the first director general. The Indus Velley civilization was discovered in 1922-23. Excavations were conducted at many sites like Taxila, Patliputra, Sanchi etc. Site museums were set up and scholars could embark on unearthing Indian History properly.

Initially agriculture and handicrafts were totally neglected but on account of general suffering and strident famines, a department of agriculture was set up in 1871 and the growing of cash crops encouraged for British planters. For the upkeep of draught animals especially army mules, the Imperial Veterinary Research Institute was established at Izatnagar U.P. initially as a branch of the Imperial Bacteriological Labortary, Mukteshwar and the first veterinary college was established at Lahore in 1882. Work in soil sciences, entomology, and plant pathology was begun by British workers J.W. Leather, Harold Maxwell-defroy and E.J. Bullen respectively around the turn of the century who also wrote books on rotation of crops and drainage, insect pests, and fungel diseases. In 1911 the Indian Research Fund Association was created to promote scientific medical research in India. It carried out very successful studies on malnutrition, malaria, rabies, plague, cholera, leprosy and kala azar. The work of the association was taken over by Indian Council of Medical Research after independence. Famous British researchers were Ronald Ross (malaria), Paul Symond (plague bacillus) and Haffikins (plague vaccine).

4. The U.S. concern

During the war years there was pressure of the United States on the British for promising independence to India engaged in the liberation struggle. Indians tended to count on American sympathy on account of Americans' own earlier struggle for independence and their democratic professions and love of liberty. The American public has often displayed idealism in international affairs. The U.S. food aid at the time of India's need after independence was very timely. India however expected liberal technological assistance for growth especially from U.S.A. since India's political posture, they thought, was closest to that of democratic United States. But all along India was bewildered by the American lukewarm policies in this regard. Perhaps the Americans had burnt their fingers in China where they gave considerable aid to the chiang Kai Shek government which was overthrown by the communists who were very close apparantly at that time to the Soviet Union. There was gratuitous equation of India irrespective of its size, population and ideals with Pakistan following the discredited British policy of balance of power by fraternal conflicts in South Asia. The independent stand of India on international issues and attempts at non-alignment which is now the established policy of the majority of nations, was considered inimical to U.S. interests that sought military alliances. The planning of a large public sector in India was regarded as opposed to the American theology about private sector and private profit. The United States was obviously attempting a status quo in the advancement of large countries like India and had no use for a new power to take shape in this part of the world. The American policies were also doctrinnaire. Democracy was equated to private profit. For giving a green signal to private investments from U.S.A. in India, they desired acceptable safe-guards against nationalisation and continued guarantee for repatriation of profits. The Indians desired the private investments to be part of a plan and not for exploitation of cheaper Indian labour for multiplication of consumer goods. India also wished to oversee genuine transfer of resources and know-how. Still large private investments did take place in consumer industries and led to repatriation of considerable profits for rather elementary technologies. Notable investments have been in production of cosmetics, patent medicines, refrigeration equipment, air-craft industries, manufacture of telegraph and telephone equipments, polymer industry and manufacture of synthetic fibres etc. The well known industrial houses in the country have hundreds of minor know-how agreements with foreign interests. The success of such agreements and their mutual profitability have now attracted even the U.S.S.R. state enterprises to deal also with the Indian private sector. India obviously welcomes mutually profitable industrial growth whether in the public sector or in the complementary private sector. Just after the war, and in the wake of considerable goodwill on account of Indian independence and the American public support to it, most American universities and institutions opened their portals to Indian students and scholars in technical studies. Hundreds were trained to the top level of their education, often assisted by Fullbright and Ford Foundation financial aid, who on return to India manned most of the development agencies and projects along with some others who managed their training in the war-ravaged institutions of England and Europe. Amrican contribution to the advancement of agricultural research, management education, oceanographay, meteorology and environmental sciences has been considerable in the form of exchange of information and experts e.g. Prof. E.C. LaFond from San Diego for oceanography and Roger Revelle for Engineering etc. In addition may expatriate Indian scientists, now often U.S. citizens, often visit Indian scene for lecture tours and advisory roles e.g. Dr. Pran Vohra for setting up the first modern poultry farm in the Punjab.

5. Growth of modern technology

In 1935, under provincial autonomy, popular governments with limited powers were established in India and Jawaharlal Nehru had begun his non-official exercise in planned economic development. Village industries received considerable support. Gandhiji's constructive programme became local policy. Agricultural and industrial schools received encouragement. At the time of the outbreak of the war it became evident that India must develope as quickly as possible to assist the allied war effort meaningfully. The technical scene was dismal. Most of the graduates of universities and engineering colleges were engaged in sales and maintenance jobs or worked in administration. No machine tools or vehicles were made in India. There was very little to boast of except the textile and jute industries. There was only some token production of iron and steel, petroleum refining, chemicals or drugs to meet the stunted economy needs. During war-time the government supported production of all kinds of stores in the country like cement, chemicals, drugs, iron, rubber etc. etc. A council of Scientific and Industrial Research was set up which drew up plans for a number of national laboratories and their nuclei started functioning in existing universities and other scientific institutions. Many industrial research projects were sponsored and many small engineering units were established. The expansion of industrial manufacture really started after independence when the public sector could begin planned development initially with the timely assistance of the socialist countries.

6. Railway and Defence Equipment

In the early days the British encouraged defence stores to be manufactured in the country especially when the regular supply from U.K. might be delayed and large scale stock piling in the country may not be feasible. Indian technicians were already available for the casting of guns, and making of swords and saddles or wooden boats and sailing ships. Some Indian made ships saw service with the East India Company. The ancient gun and ammunition factories in Calcutta, Pune or Kanpur represent the beginning of Defence Industries in India and the beginnings of the Public Sector. After independence, self-reliance meant that the defence production in the country would be a foremost objective. In the famous words of Jawaharlal Nehru, a country must fight with the weapons she can produce even if these are only bows and arrows than rely over much on imported ones with precarious dependence on others for spares and maintenance items. The accent on heavy industries was also a step in the same direction. At present there are a large number of ordnance factories distributed all over India. Other well known industries engaged in defence production are Hindustan Aircraft Ltd, Ship Building yards at Calcutta and Bombay, Kirloskar Engines, Tractor manufacturers, Tank, missile and alloy factories etc. etc. The annual defence production is a sizeable percentage of the total industrial production. India has unilaterally eschewed the manufacture of nuclear weapons, though it has the capacity as was evident from the 1974 atomic explosion carried out as an experiment for possible peaceful uses of such explosions. India has no nuclear submarines and nor has countermeasures against such a menace. (It is understood that nuclear depth charges are perhaps the only countermeasures.) In the matter of missiles, India is totally dependent on imports, excepting for some primitive anti-tank missiles. The defence R&D organisation, it seems, has done considerable home-work in the absorption of possible imported technologies. They have tinkered with improvements in existing weapon systems and in working out system performance or in avoiding unnecessary frills. Considerable experience in rocket technology and electronics has been built up during the development of electronic warfare and countermeasure devices and concepts. The civilian space effort has also developed technical know-how. In 1986, an Indian rocket is scheduled to place an Indian satellite in orbit. Considerable experience already exists in the design and the use of satellites.

Good communications were necessary for holding the Indian empire together. The main pillar of good communications in the colonial days was the railway organisation which was the foremost carrier of passengers and goods. Most of the rolling stock and engines were imported, along with almost the entire sensitive equipment. The first track was planned for Calcutta to Raniganj and executed in 1854, while in 1853 a track was laid between Thana (Bombay) and Pune. Howra-Delhi trains started in 1866. By 1873 most of the railway network had been completed, extending over 63000 km. The enterprise was carried out by private British companies with liberal aid and assistance from the government of India. The nationalisation of the railways started in 1925 and was completed in 1944. The entire system including the few companies in erstwhile princely states became Indian National Railways in 1950.

Some enterprising railway managements started indigenous production of railway equipment. Few railway engines were actually built in the maintenance workshops at Ajmer and Gwalior. Such efforts established a trained core of technicians when the Chittaranjan Loco Works was set up in 1950. An integral coach factory was set up. By now India has not only become self-sufficient in the manufacture of railway equipment, but can also export both equipment and know-how to other developing countries. The Railway Design and Research Organisation at Lucknow is in the fore-front of similar organisations in connection with railway technology. They keep in touch with developments in the country or abroad. They have helped many Indian industries to meet the needs of Indian railways.

7. Growth of public sector

For capital intensive industries with long gestation periods and for essential heavy industries the natural planner and investor in an under-developed country is the state. The growth of public sector in India is more from practical benefits than from considerations of ideology. The state could also keep in view the national interest much better than private owners when dealing with foreign interests for essential imports and exports as well as import of know-how. There also was ample opportunity in less capital intensive consumer industries giving quick returns for the Indian private sector, immediately after the world war. From India's long range security and self-reliance it was essential that basic industries be given top priority even if this was counter to the advice of friends in the west, who believed in international sharing of production leaving simpler consumer articles for the third world and perhaps keeping it dependent on the advanced countries for ever. The planning priority was not appreciated by England and America who were first sounded for technical and financial assistance. This was the situation when the Soviet Union came to the rescue of the Indian planners and the efforts of India to become self reliant. The setting up of heavy industries and modern steel and oil industries is primarily due to Russian assistance. Afterwards other countries of the West also were amenable to enter into development agreements, and they also contributed to the establishment of some basic production plants. India is now almost surplus in steel, fertilizers, oil refining capacity, cement etc. The internal as well as external demand is however continuously rising and further expansion is still necessary. Most of the public sector industries in the past have grown on imported equipment and imported know-how. Only now the further expansion of the public sector is utilising considerable Indian equipment and already assimilated and modified know-how. Some technologists have all along felt that some-what slower growth of the public sector primarily based on Indian technological growth might have brought self-reliance much nearer. Even now major developments in the production processes are occurring abroad and many of our costly factories are already outdated since imported equipment and know how usually is decades old. Only now at a very late stage on account of mounting difficulties in meeting international competition, the government run industrial research and national laboratories so far ploughing their lonely furrows, are being integrated for problem solving of specific public sector industries. Even in the defence public sector, the use of Indian defence research establishments had only been peripheral, since the immediate priority demand was insisted for highly sophisticated well advertised weapon systems far ahead of the current work of the Indian researchers. For any future weapon system requirements we must plan about 15 years ahead and then see the system through to completion and authorization. On the other hand the qualitative requirements seemed to change with the advertisements in the glossy armament industry brochures and apparently authentic test reports, issued by the manufacturers in association with some pocket army or the other. When the research workers almost on their own using lean resources did manage to offer some useful weapon or system, the users had no confidence in themselves to try the same or to accept it and to authorize it. The whole project would end in smoke created by all kinds of trials, retrials, and then further trials till the foreign advertisers had something similar off the shelf for which they claimed the users need go to no trouble. But recently it is gathered that users as well as researchers have benefitted from experience and long range development funds have become available with guaranteed initial production and the researchers, users and inspectors as well as manufacturers jointly try to minimise hurdles than trying to create them. The following industries seem to have properly integrated research teams with the production efforts : alloys, radar and communications, heavy machines, vehicles, engineering materials etc.

A real success story is that of the Oil and Natural Gas Commission initially based on imported technology. Reserves of oil and gas have been established that should make India entirely self sufficient by 1990. During the last years, 800 million tons of oil equivalent reserves have been established. The production of crude oil has reached 26 million tons with current rate of increase at 13% per annum. New drilling over land has now begun. In addition isolated offshore productive oil wells have been located in the Bay of Bengal and export surplus may be soon possible.

There seems to be diffidence in planners for accepting the logic of growth of self-reliance. Indian defence research establishments have been in the forefront of international advances in the area of corrosion and corrosion protection and supervising cathodic portection of dozens of underground structures or naval installations and vessels, but recently there is a news item of the import of cathodic protection technology of under ground pipelines from an American firm. Such work should have been awarded to Indian consulants who could draw on Indian research and production capacities which is abundant in this field. There should be correct advice available to higher executives. In this technological age, it would be quite in order to have suitable attachment for few weeks of selected youth leaders and budding politicians to staff colleges where resources of the country in materials, energy and skills can be authoritatively learnt by them and they get to know the organizational structures that must be drawn upon for national development. Repeated or non essential imports must be allowed only under exceptional circumstances.

8. Energy and power

In the last fifty years, there has been a revolution in the scale of energy production and new energy resources have been identified and harnessed to varying extent. Earlier, only larger cities had electrical power. There were also certain well known hydroelectric schemes in operation, but only a fraction of the hydrolectric potential had been realised. None of the villages had electricity, common people even in cities were innocent of the existence of electric power. Buildings or even monuments rarely had lifts, cloth fans pulled by muscle power were in vogue, Earthen pitchers cooled water for drinking and the age-old use of solar energy for drying of daily wash or for drying of fish or agricultural produce was carried out in the open without any scientific considerations of efficiency. The most efficient use of solar energy is in the growth of plants but scientific development and spread of agriculture or forestry was not being attempted. The scene has changed tremendously. There is now rural electrification covering already more than half of the total number of villages. Electric fans and refrigerators have entered almost all middle class homes. Great strides have been made in the efficient functiong of agriculture, forestry, sheep farming and animal husbandry, all dependent so much on the harnessing and husbanding of the solar energy resource. In the last ten years we have become exporters of grains from having been importers earlier. The export of plants including garden plants, herbs, decorative and fruit trees has become a lucrative industry for some. There is now a well deserved emphasis on the social forestry since the forest cover has been reduced to a level much below the minimum necessary for human habitat. Rural supply of fire wood has to be deliberately augmented by planting fast growing trees. Recent development of bio-gas generation using human and animal wastes, and agricultural wastes, is also ensuring reliable fuel and manure to villagers. The government is supporting the spread of biogas plants. Use of solar heat for cooking is also being assisted by government subisidy. High technology in solar energy is also entering villages in the form of silicon cells for lighting and providing power for the community sets especially in remote places. As experimental models, energy resources like ocean tides and ocean thermal gradient are also being harnessed.

Most heartening has been the use of low quality coal in thermal power stations and the extraction of crude from offshore. On account of recent successes in oil exploration, extraction and refining, kersoene and gas are the fuels of choice in most urban homes. Most of the irrigation pumps and road traffic including haulage of goods by road are now dependent on diesel. Many railway engines use diesel. The development of fluidized bed coal furnances is likely to save much coal. A five megawtt MHD electric generator developed by Bharat Heavy Electricals is a development of international importance towards efficient generation of electricity. Soviet experience of underground gassification of coal is under study for use in certain coal beds in India.

By the end of the next five year plan, coal output will cross 200 million ton mark, the power generating capacity will be doubled to more than forty billion megawatts. India has become self-sufficient in the design and construction of complete power plants and has begun exporting the same along with the know-how. The indigenous extraction of crude meets about 70% of current requirements and Indian refineries meet the full home requirements. While the present requirements amount to 33 million tons, the need will rise to about sixty million tons in another five years and will be met by own production. The major portion of the expanding gas production will be diverted to the production of fertilizers. After setting up coal washeries of better design, the abundant low quality coal could also be converted to more fertilizers and chemicals. Most of the power generation is in the public sector. Industry is however encouraged now to set up captive plants. The demand of electric power at present outstrips the available power which is also reflected in frequent power cuts in cities to augment the supplies to agriculture sector. Besides various energy resources from water and coal, major augmentation is expected from atomic power.

9. Atomic energy

Indian scientists were quite alive to the potential of atomic energy for peace. A department of Atomic Energy has been set up usually under the stewardship of the Prime Minister himself. We have now many reactors producing electric power and isotopes as well as some reactors for research purposes including research on thorium as fuel, research for carbide fuels and research for breeder reactors. Canadian assistance for design and development of atomic reactors ceased when India exploded a nuclear device for possible peaceful purposes in 1974.

India has been in the fore-front of movements for abandonment of nuclear weapons. She has however refused to sign the nuclear non-proliferation treaty since this treaty does not hinder vertical proliferation and the current international tensions concerning disarmament are due to the limited horizons of this troaty. Partly on this account the U.S.A stopped supplies of enriched fuel elements for the Tarapore reactor for which they had initially contracted and even sent supplies earlier. Perforce India had to seek alternate fuels and were able to run successfully the reactor on mixed carbide fuel, which is regarded as a breakthrough for self-reliance and the new fuel could also use abundant thorium resources in the country.

The power units are being designed in units of 200 MWe or 500 MWe output. By the year 2000 A.D. the power production is expected to be from atomic means, 10,000 MWe i.e. 10% of total capacity in the country. Breeder reactors will allow the second phase of atomic energy expansion programme in the coming decade.

The atomic energy department has been extremely successful in their many activities. They have located and developed atomic minerals and carried out metallurgical operations and produced feeder alloy rods as well as control rods. Recently they have developed in the country the reactor end-shields. Almost all the pumps and heavy machinery as well as instrumenutation is now designed and developed in the country. They are in a position to assist in the setting up and supply of atomic reactors. Many heavy water plants have been set up. For becoming adept in advanced instrumentation, they carried out pioneering developments in the country for introducing new technologies like modern welding, chemical machining, computerisation of machines and processes. On the basis of their experimental instrument designs, the Electrical Corporation of India was set up at Hyderabad that are manufactuting and marketing many electronic instruments, computers and consumer items. The atomic energy department is also engaged in designing and operating service for transportation of atomic minerals, waste disposal, health monitoring, nuclear medicine, production and supplies of isotopes and labelled compounds etc.

The atomic energy department has also not neglected basic research especially in nuclear physics. The major institutions for basic research are the Tata Institute of Fundamental Research in Bombay and Saha Institute of Nuclear Physics at Calcutta. Recently a new university research centre is being planned at J.N. University at Delhi for basic nuclear research, besides a centre for emerging technologies at Bhopal. The Tata institute is engaged in fundamental research. They are using Kolar Gold Mines for carrying out proton decay experiments at great depths. They have contributed to research on cosmic rays including designing the payload for satellites. The main atomic energy research centre is the Bhabha Atomic Research Centre at Trombay. Research reactors are operating at Trombay and Madras. Energy is produced at Tarapur, Kota and Kalpakkam. Boiling water reactors with 71% availability are under construction at Narora, Kakrapar, Heavy water plants are beginning production at Talcher, Nangal, Baroda, Manugura, Tuticorin, Kota, Thal Vashisht etc. An experimental MHD generator is being set up near Madras.

BARC has been duplicating many advanced technologies and transferring know-how and expertise to Indian manufacturers and technicians through an intensive training programme and technical consultancy arrangents, e.g. laser technology, cryogenics, electronic and computer centred instruments, design, erection and operation of reactors and particle machines, gamma radiography, preparation and use of isotopes and labelled compounds, radiation medicine, health physics, waste disposal desalination plants, etc. Hundreds of new jobs and new downstream enterprises have been established as a result of scientific and technical achievements of this department. Eminent scientists like Bhabha, Menon and Ramanna, Yash Pal and others have been associated with some of the work.

Among the high-lights could be mentioned thorium production (1955), critcality of first Asian reactor Apsara (1956), Cirus Reactor with Indian made fuel elements (1960), recovery of U^{233} from irradiated thorium (1970), plutonium-uramium mixed oxide fuel fabricated (1979), mixed carbide fuel for fast breeder research reactor fabricatd (1984), Waste immobilization plant at Tarapur (1985), Madras Atomic power station II (1985) and criticality of FBTR (October 1985).

10. Private sector

In technology, the private sector in India was an extension of foreign industries. Here and there some farseeing Indians developed industries on their own initiative using Indian khow-how for example the drugs and chemical industries especially based around Calcutta. But by and large turnkey plants were imported from U.K. or Germany or other western countries. Most of the raw materials or the intermediates and all process or quality control instruments were either identified proprietary products from abroad or were specified as per the foreign country's products so that local stores could not meet the needs particularly since guarantee clauses bound the Indian entrepreuner. The investment was made by foreign interests in the form of machinery, materials and know-how. Management also stayed in the hands of the foreign interests, or of Indians paid handsomely to work in their interest. After independence foreign personnel got displaced but policies in such industries remained the same. The private sector was given many concessions by the government after independence and it was allowed to expand in many directions not reserved for the public sector. The slow rate of industrialization was in the past due to deficiencies in managerial and entrepreunerial skills. There was initial carelessness in the import of machinery and know-how and then technological incompetence to adapt the know-how to locally available materials and equipment. Half the time entrepreneurship consisted in short-cuts to profiteering and slowly the reputation of Indian equipment dropped compared to the imported one. Some of the troubles arose because institutional involvement of Indian consultants and R&D workers was not carried out. Conditions in this respect are now better. Many Indian engineering consultancy groups have come of age the hard way after making lot of avoidable mistakes under the tutelage of certain vested interests in India and abroad. Best assistance for self-reliance has come from the socialist countries both in the philosophy of self-help and building forward from what one has got, and in the exercise of technical judgement from basic engineering data. Most of the private sector is so used to spoon feeding of technology that they hardly contribute to the building up of design data by actıng partially as experimental factories. This has however, been accomplished to some extent by the textile, jute, woollen, and sugar industries. The common R&D units like the Textile Research Associtation Laboratories or the National Sugar Research Institue have been very helpful in allowing the industry to become self-reliant. Many industries still do not consult available talent on their corrosion and packaging problems. Some of the technology in the private sector is such as could be picked up from foreign brochures and samples by technicians. Such technology can hardly grow and prosper in international competition to which Indian products must now get exposed more and more.

Licensed production and import of advanced technology or advanced machines and instruments are not to be halted. These are almost necessary for all countries in the present day world of unheard of technological advancement. What is not to be tolerated is the repeated import of technology of almost same standard for same or allied products and not building ahead on the technology once imported. The private sector must learn to limit their declared as well as undeclared profits. They must be conscious about the quality and efficiency and rely more on truth than wrong notion about "business" lack of ethics. The artificial environment of protection and profiteering trade in materials and products is not likely to be tolerated by the public for long.

The Indian firms compete on the strength of their ability to acquire know-how and managerial ability usually from foreign sources. There is the spectacle of proprietors and industrial managers periodically visiting their Japanese or British Meccas to pick up common items from their markets and offering know-how tie-ups to almost anyone there for common knowledge but incidentally binding themselves to specifications suiting established sources of materials, equipment and instruments in those countries. The foreign well wishers, too, often laugh at such illiterate behaviour. The Indian industrialist saves however his own time and energy in planning and location of sources within the country, but then he faces all kinds of delays in bureaucratic allocations or delays in construction. Often the imported machinery stays idle for the entire guarantee period and then he has to pay for further repairs and modifications or look around for local talents which he disdained at start. He tends to depend on cheap technicians rather than higher scientific and engineering skills available in the country. Only recently scientists and engineers in the national and public institutions have been accepted as possible practitioners of their professions privately in their own time as was expected from physicians. Many scientists and engineers in our universities, I am sure will measure up well if only the entrepreuners learn to reach them. The institutions are now coming forward to encourage consultancy by their teaching and research faculties. This has been standard practice in Europe and America. Project planning and supervision need not be left to improvisation entirely. Another possible measure would be to encourage serving scientists and engineers to openly espouse personal or cooperative industries which can also assist in student employment towards practical experience. Many well known industrial giants in USA and Japan started in this manner.

In India, an innovative experiment of cooperative endeavour by working scientists, though a success on all accounts, was nipped in the bud by the technologist bureaucrats under the politicians' plea that when R&D scientists paid by Government set up an industry, they are in a relatively priveleged position compared to ordinary entrepreneures from the public, and so they cannot be allowed to do so ! This kind of logic is possible only in a doctrinnaire socialist society where any initiative can be discouraged if everyone else is not having the same environment ! In U.S.A., a university lecturer is applauded if he can simultaneously be a director in a firm, a bank, or an advertisement firm, but here the conditions of service debar one for any other productive initiative, I am sure, under the false plea that this means occupying more remunerative positions than can be one's legitimate share in a destitute economy, a type of argument trade unions have against recognition of multiple skills. We must give up archaic and negative aspects of trade unionism and short-sighted interpretation of socialism, e.g., equal distribution of inefficiency and inaction. Every individual must be permitted to grow to his full potential. Let there be more production and profits, and individuals can always be taxed or brain-washed to give in charity or hold in trust the surplus earned by him.

The small scale sector which is mostly in private hands has

grown to four times its size a decade ago, and is now showing a production worth Rs. 10,000 crores at 1971 prices. The number of units have almost doubled. Many public sector industries have set up ancillaries in small scale sector or have bulk-purchase-of-production agreements with them. For the small scale sector, major bottleneck is marketing of product and the procurement of appropriate quality raw materials. The Government may have to attend to these difficulties in the manner they have now started assisting the agricultural sector. The production must be inadequate to meet the genuine needs of the immense population which is below the poverty line. If the product is socially supplied to the masses, the private sector can develope to heights unimaginable at present. To make them competitive, they must be cajoled or compelled to export a fraction of their product, by improving quality and cutting costs to meet international competition when the procurement delays and protected market do not allow foreign products to compete within the country. The government functionaries within the country or in the embassies abroad should have a brief to expand the markets for Indian products. The spread of the private small scale sector into the villages alone has the potential of solving India's problem of poverty and unemployment and incidentally reverse the trend of migration to cities which is stifling the growth of the Indian society.

Almost the entire agriculture and handicrafts sectors constitute another aspect of private enterprise. The distribution of land to the tillers and proliferous financial loans to individual artisans for owning and improving the tools of their trade have been of great assistanee. Agriculture and orchards tied to large scale private food processing industries are only begining to grow.

11. Scientific education

In 1813, the East India Company budgeted a small amount for imparting British style of education to Indians. Indian reformers like Raja Ram Mohan Roy and certain Christian missions initiated Eŭropean education covering English literature, philosophy and Modern Science along with other subjects. After Lord Macaulay's views were accepted in 1835, it became British policy to start departments of public instruction in each state and set up universities for education in English medium, for subjects like science, western literature and philosophy. In the beginning of the 20th Contury, major cities had universities and professional colleges including colleges for medicine and engineering. Medical degree of the Calcutta University was recognized in U.K. in 1892. The Roorkee Engineering College was set up in 1847. Some industrial and agricultural schools were also set up.

The Indian Association for the Cultivation of Science was set up by Mahendralal Sircar in 1876 for instruction and research, and C.V. Raman N.L. and K.S. Krishnan worked in its laboratories (Science College, Calcutta). Bose Research Institute was set up by Prof. Jagadish Chandra Bose in 1917 in Calcutta. Many stalwarts of Indian Science were produced by the Calcutta Institutions like M.N. Saha, S.N. Bose, J.C. Ghosh, J.N. Mukherjee, N.R. Dhar and P.C, Ray and many others. But all over India innumerable teachers of science, mathematics and English were initially British teachers followed by many Indians qualified from Oxford, Cambridge, London and Dublin Universities.

Quite a few prestigious research institutes were started: Imperial Agricultural Research Institute at Pusa in 1903 (shifted to New Delhi in 1935), Central Medical Research Institute, Imperial Dairy Research Institute, Bangalore in 1920, Pasteur Institute, Conoor 1907, Indian Institute of Science, Bangalore 1911, Indian Statistical Institute 1931, Railway Research and Design Centre, Lucknow and Central Water and Power Commission Research Station, Pune etc. etc. Many Science, societies and academies were set up with Indian National Science Academy at their apex (started in 1934 as the National Institute of Sciences). Funds are available from various agencies like the Department of Science and Technology and the University Grant Commission for research projects in universities etc.

The trained manpower was increased manifold during the war years. Skilled technicians were required in large numbers in the armed forces, technicians for maintenance and repairs of trucks, ships and aircraft were now available. An Indian scientist independently discovered nuclear fission (Prof. S.D. Chatterjee) but on account of war-time secrecy and lack of contact with German and American work, the importance of his observations was not realised. Prof. Bhabha and his colleagues in the Tata Institute of Fundamental Research made considerable advances in nuclear Physics.

The educational system is now under review. The employers must design practical training in association with governmental and other bodies for the specific needs of young men of certain basic general education in science, arts and crafts after their selection. The advanced education should be possible by continuing education, open universities and correspondence courses. Only a few top class motivated young men may pursue advanced university education for careers in R&D. In addition there has to be a means for assuring mobility of scientific and engineering manpower depending on the changing needs of employers and society. The areas of economic and social importance must receive more attention by the educational institutions like manufacturing technology, geology and mining, electro-chemistry, building technology, recreation technology etc. Universities should encourage patentable work in their departments as well as development of new instruments. The art of self reliance, resourcefulness and solving problems should be strengthened among the students at all levels. This can be done by dedicated teachers who can guide the students in their projects and in allowing the younger students more time to think and discuss among themselves as well as with their seniors. This is not possible so long as the accent is on burdening the young minds with more data that can easily be dug up in future from programmed computors. The spectacle of small children carrying a donkey's load of books etc to school and engaging in needless bookish homework day after day is so disappointing.

Science and Technology are so much identified with the English language, that it will take decades to propagate science among the masses of India in an idiom which is native to them. The question is bedevilled by the unthinking prejudice against forging a single science language for the country that will become the language for all thinking Indians as happened through the spread of Sanskrit in ancient times, or of Prakrit in Buddhist days or of Bhakti language (apbhransh) of saints in the middle ages. The adult edueation is being attempted in regional languages and Hindi happens to be the language of the majority of people, but any effort to make it the common language of science is not likely to succeed. A new seientific Indian language has to evolve perhaps in Roman script often using English terms. The structure of the language and other words will be mostly the ones in common usage in India i.e. a mixture of Hindi, Bengali, Tamil etc. words. This language should be such as can be the vehicle of scientific temper for the common people anywhere in India just as film songs are understood almost all over India in whatever idiom these are sung. The structure of the new language will closely follow that of Hindi and Tamil which together cover all the veriations of grammer in Indian languages. Such a scientiflc 'Indian' language can be conveniently forged by using it in Defence forces as Roman Urdu was used by the British and then extending it to Railways, post-offices and hospitals. Any new institute of higher education must begin with the new language as medium of instruction for the sciences.

12. Conclusion

Modern science and technology was introdued in India before independence. Outstanding individuals and small groups were active in almost all the basic sciences and many kinds of technicians were available on account of war-time needs. There were however shortcomings in both quality and quantity in almost all areas. The problems facing India were of dire poverty, ill health, food scarcity, leaping population, need for imports and dearth of new exports etc. Most of the trained technical manpower was engaged in routine work or teaching. Enterprise consisted in trade and profiteering. People were so used to the import of finished goods or turnkey plants that innovative change was missing. Self reliance in certain fields was never expected. The industrial scene was most disquieting. The scientific community was practically cut off from the practical problems of innovation and production. Excepting the few scintillating stars of Indian science that shone now and then, great successes proportional to the trained manpower in the country were missing. The social advantages of science for the betterment of human intellect that is inherent through science, remained mostly a promise only. Even the people trained in science were affected by the environment of greed and injustice, scarcity and unemployment, to be hardly objective in their assessment of persons and proposals.

5

INDUSTRIALIZATION OF INDIA

1. Imported industrialization

The industrialization of the Western countries had taken centuries. Forced and planned industrialization of Russia took place as a part of the Western world. The sufferings that these countries underwent during their industrialization whether as capitalist countries or whether as communist ones. were not considered essential for present day development of India who would benefit from the European experience. India was naturally keen to industrialize quickly since that alone would raise the standard of her millions or make it possible for her to feel secure in the modern world. India also had chalked out for herself the policy of non-alignment since in the absence of economic strength, she could live at peace with herself only if there was non-alignment since in alignment with stronger countries, there would be compulsion to play a secondary role. The West did not feel close enough to non-aligned India, to give her assistance for industrial progress as they were doing for the European or the erstwhile enemy countries like Germany or Japan. Soviet Union also preferred to build industries in China which was regarded as a fraternal communist nation. Soon China was manufacturing heavy machinery and armaments including atom bombs and the equipment and designs had come from the Soviet Union.

West was also partial to the then British view of India. India had scuttled the empire and presumably harboured revolutionaries and leftists. The British also desired to retard her growing strength by keeping a power balance through much smaller but aligned Pakistan. The British hoped to keep Pakistan or India at the level of development of the Arab lands. The west regarded the Islamic states as preferable to secular states that were potentially perhaps stronger. India was keen to step up production quickly recognising the critical situation of public expectations after independence. The West was willing to offer technical and financial aid for import of food, for village uplift, and for communications. India was advised to scale down the industrial ambitions and concentrate on becoming an exporter of agricultural produce, minerals and raw materials or perhaps jute and cotton textiles. For setting up industries the West could do so where it was profitable and the profitability was immense at no risk in consumer industries like cosmetics and drugs. Soon, profits many times the initial investments were carted away from such industries as the manufacture of tooth paste and shaving gear etc. This kind of industrialization hardly brought employment opportunities or self-reliance nearer. At this juncture the situation took an interesting turn and the Soviet Union attempted to give meaning to their slogans that the strength of the Soviet Union meant development for all poor countries and the Indian leaders also swore by the world view of anticolonialism and supremacy of public sector in basic and critical production. In order to save Indian economy from further dependence on the West the Soviet Union came forward to help India set up heavy industries. The Soviet link was the first major step towards development of India. The transfer of resources and know-how and later the buy back arrangements of some of the new products were the best any developed country could accord a developing country, consistent with the aim to help it to help itself.

2. Reorientation of Indian thinking

Before mentioning in detail the assistance in Industrialization received from other countries and discussing the role of multinationals, one must understand that ultimately self-reliance has to come from a creative and innovative approach to even copying and learning. For the grafted technology to flourish, the sap of dedication and objective approach must be applied to it. Indian mind had made great perceptions and discoveries in the past. What were the sources of its strength ? Any light thrown on this might illuminate our future course as well. The Greek philosophers and the Indian seers enquired about the interrelationships of mind and matter, man and nature and about the ultimate reality. An ideal man in India was taken as one who would have evenness of temper and who will perform his duties with detachment, he will also tread the path of truth. Acquisition of strength of purpose was recognised to happen through meditation, prayer and vows. Man's worth was not counted by his possessions, but by his knowledge and virtue. Knowledge however had become argumentative with citation of authority almost as the scientists now do. Logical deductions not supported by Vedic authority were regarded as heresy, though most of the people then and even now integrated the Buddhist and Jain heresies within their wide net of beliefs. These advances were beyond their times. Jains had believed in probabilstic composite reality. Buddhists had very much modern ideas on the objective reality of consciousness. Bertrand Russell's exhortation to mankind to learn to live with ambiguity in the present scientific age of suspended judgement is a clear echo of the Jain teaching of yore. India invented a very close almost filial relationship between the student and the teacher. The teacher revelled in the success of the pupil and the pupil gave him devotion and reverence. Perhaps this later deteriorated to blind acceptance of authoritative statements so inimical to enquiry and scientific advance. A good teacher always encourages the pupil to ask questions for which we have examples both in Greek as well as in Indian ancient texts. Buddha always taught by discussing problems that were first identified. There must have been some inhibition from questioning empirical data available about practical matters like medicine, metallurgy or astrology. People continued to add to empirical knowledge without developing insights for common properties in different chemicals and chemistry never advanced beyond alchemie. The lightning was explained as a weapon of a god though they seem to have empirically hit upon the use of the lightning conductor. One suspects that more energy was spent on virtuous living and virtue included careful memorising and sacrificial use of scriptures. Even Buddhists and Jains spent large amount of time on reading their voluminous sacred lore than on discussions about possible improvements in their philosophies. A society is influenced by the rewards and punishments it ordains. Perhaps the higher social returns and better self-image were granted for the meticulous performance of the sacred rituals, recitation of scriptures or hair-splitting arguments about non-issues like the exact progress of the soul after death. The desired directions in human progress should be reflected in the rewards etc.

With the ancient Indians, the lack of material possessions was often considered a virtue. It was evidently not a consumer oriented society but one where piety included reduction of needs. We may have to reorient our thinking towards the middle path of reasonable possessions for modern day simple living. In those days school subjects were more often grammer and poetry and not properties of matter etc. Any cultured man even in the eighteenth century only wrote poetry and cultivated being a gentlement in politeness and chivalry. Thus for fresh breeze of creative processess to blow, there was need to encourage once again the questioning of authority and give respect to the learned who could apply their knowledge to development of useful products and processes. The abject suffering and poverty on the one hand and example of progress in the West based on science and technology gave confidence that India will also change its direction for providing adequate living to her citizens and the people will deliver what was expected from them.

3. Soviet aid for heavy industries

The agreement on economic cooperation was signed between the Soviet Union and India in 1955. India did this after knocking at the chanceries of the West for about a decade where it was expounded that the heavy industry should be left to private sector and in any case should have lower priority. The first steel plant at Bhilai was set up under the agreement involving rouble credit equivalent to Rs. 650 million at that time. There were no strings attached to this credit. The Russians also agreed to set up a training institute for steel making in India and there were provisions for exchange of trainees and teachers.

After the successful launching of the steel project there were many more advanced projects begun with Russian assistance. Mention may be made of the heavy machine building plant at Ranchi, Opthalmic glass factory at Durgapur, The Neyweli thermal power plant, the Central Electrical and Mechanical

Workshop at Korba and some coal mining projects. In 1959, the Soviet Union helped the drug and pharmaceutical industry by setting up an antibiotics plant at Rishikesh and Surgical Instruments Plant at Hyderabad ; in addition many other plants were also established, e.g. Bhakra hydro-power station, Electrical equipment manufacture at Hardwar etc. The Soviet Union provided the know-how and the enterprise for the initial offshore exploration for oil that has now made India practically self-sufficient for crude. They also helped set up the Instrument factory at Kota, and the Brauni Oil Refinery in Bihar. The Soviet aided projects account for 36 per cent of total steel production in India, 26 per cent of Aluminium, 25 per cent oil and 45 per cent oil refining, 70 per cent of metallurgical equipment, 43 per cent of mining equipment and 54 per cent power equipment manufactured in the country. For re-payment, India was allowed to export consumer items in barter. This incidentally helped consumer industries in India to have an easy access to a large foreign market. This trade has expanded still more when the Soviet customers have started dealing with the Indian private sector for supplies conforming to their foreign designs and specifications. In 1971, with all this background of economic cooperation and other mutually beneficial cooperation, India and the Soviet Union entered into a treaty of friendship and cooperation and Russian know-how was made available even for industries like defence, space or computors. The Russian aided institutions and industries are entirely managed by Indians and are shining example of the socialist style of international cooperation between nations having different social, economic and political systems.

4. International assistance

Due to an enlightened interest in universal development through sharing of resources and know-how with the developing countries, many developed countries and international bodies like those of United Nations have set up programmes of international assistance. The United States have also set up aid programmes directed towards certain selected countries and projects through government agencies or between private parties and American foundations. Many other countries have offered aid on government to government basis. The Colombo plan has channelised similar aid between commonwealth countries. Training is offered through visits of teachers or of students. Practical training in factories and management situations is provided. One expects considerable transfer of technology through the newly established South Asian Regional Cooperation body by the countries of South Asia including India and Pakistan.

The Canadian assistance to the Indian Nuclear Power Generation was a similar effort. The purpose of the assistance was fully served when the agreement was terminated after the Indian peaceful nuclear explosion and India's reluctance to sign the non-proliferation treaty. Normally such heavy investment and production links have their own momentum and industrial cooperation is increasing with the U.S.A. and other Western countries. India as a leader of the non-aligned movement and a strong supporter of the U.N. has political differences with the U.S.A. but inspite of these, India's every endeavour is to promote friendship and just policies so far as U.S.A. is concernced.

India has been liberally assisted by the U.S.A. in many of her nation building projects, in training of Indian administrators and scientists and also initially by a gigantic food aid programme. Most of the gains by India due to this massive assistance however have been periodically wiped out by the Pakistani aggressions against India while it was consistently abetted by U.S. on account of the American blind grasp of the anti-Soviet plank. The chief hurdle to India's friendship with U.S.A. is the American preoccupation with a value assessment of India which is entirely out of phase with India's self-assessment. The growing technical cooperation with the U.S.A. is precariously dependent on the course of events in Asia over which India has little control as Asia is often being made the playground of cold war.

The Danish and the Norwegian assistance to fisheries development in India have been extremely energetic and whole hearted. Australian aid in sheep raising and the New-Zealand assistance in cattle raising are worthy of mention. There has been considerable import of know-how and equipment from socialist countries of Europe as well as the countries of the EEC. Many special technologies have come from the countries most well known for these, e.g. alloy industry and forestry from Sweden,

Colliery Equipment from Poland, Machine tools from Czechsalovakia and chemicals from West Germany etc.

5. Self-help

The imported know-how must be absorbed and made one's own as well as improved and modified. The Japanese and the West Germans seem to score in this. India ignored many times the necessary logic for self-help. Planning should not only involve location of a supplier of foreign know-how or foreign equipment or foreign licensed production, but it must often ponder in the long range for the development of certain technologies, the training of required manpower and the location of Indian consultants and equipment suppliers for the major part of a project. This kind of planning is only starting now when recently developed high technology is achieving commercial importance and any dependence on imported equipment might keep us back in distant future as well. The United Nations have prepared some draft technology transfer agreements that assure eventual self-reliance. Often turn-key projects were imported without the benefit of knowledge and training of Indian engineers and consultants and sometimes such plants were repeatedly imported. There should be proper attention given to the repair and maintenance of the plant and the supply of spares etc. at the initial planning stage. The details should be such that Indian raw materials should be acceptable and the production should begin within the guarantee period. The habits of dependence were built up so much by the dealings with Western multinationals and the like that the Russian principals had to chide the Indian managers for rushing with their simple enquiries to them when the Russians happened to be aware that the answers were readily available with the Indian specialists and consultants. The exporters of machinery and instruments often had guarantee clauses that inhibited any local attempts to study or improve the gadgets. After considerable losses, a policy has now been evolved for associating a suitable consultant or research group with any major import and some reduntant equipment or production capacity in India should be spared for study and experimentation. It was from experience of steel making that the first Engineering consultancy group was established. Now Indian consultancy has come of age and many international projects are being carried out by them. Some developing countries associate Indian consultants even when primarily they may be importing know-how or equipment or turnkey plants from a third country. This is a tribute to their honest endeavours in the interests of the developing country that employs them.

For building the infrastructure for indigenous know-how, Jawaharlal Nehru and S.S. Bhatnagar had conceived the setting up of many national and regional laboratories. Soon after independence the Defence Research and Development Organization was set up and it also now runs a number of research laboratories for self reliance in defence needs and to assist the armed forces and the supply organizations. In the same manner, the Council of Agricultural research and the Indian Medical Research Council have many research groups and laboratories in their respective fields. Research Institutions also have been established to assist the department of Atomic Energy and departments like ocean development, energy, mining, ministry of Industries, and some state government departments, like Police, Irrigation etc. The number of scientists and the number of research institutions is quite large but still proportionally much less than what may be optimum for the immense population and the gigantic goals. The work of the institutions is full of variety and not always directed for the innovative production. In addition the requirements of development are so vast that often research people have to be saddled also with minor engineering modifications and maintenance work requiring substitutes for common imported materials and spares. Mrs. Indira Gandhi was called the heroine of Indian Science by the editor of Nature. Under her tutelage and with her encouragement, Science in India ranged from space to Antaratica glaciers and from the study of the Himalayan ecology to the study of Deep Oceans. In the last decade government, departments dealing with electronics, environment, ocean development, space etc. have been established. A ministry for science and technology has been set up looking after certain important institutions and projects as well as for utilising the Indian emigre talents. The department of Science and Technology also looks ahead for technology development. They have panels for biotechnology, futurology, instrumentation and new sources of energy etc. The planning of expenditure on specific proposals is always carried out by the standard scientific procedure of peer review. The short-comings of the system if any are the usual personal shortcomings of individuals. One is sometimes surprised by the lack of objectivity shown by scientifically trained people. Sometimes in the prevailing situation of over-much dependence on personal likes and dislikes, certain individuals can successfully jockey themselves into key positions. Mrs. Gandhi had also commented on the lack of desired coordination at various centres of activity.

Due priorities were given to Agriculture and by 1977, India became self-sufficient in food which was a great achievement. Similarly oil exploration and refining has received priority treatment and the effort has been crowned with success. At present considerable attention is being given to coal, fisheries, electronics and non-traditional resources of energy. A science policy resolution has existed since 1951 favouring cultivation of science in all segments of society. Mrs. Gandhi formulated in 1983 a technology policy statement stressing the need for absorption and adoption of new technologies, to be committed to self-reliance in strategic and critical areas, and to restrict imports only to some well-defined selected areas.

The department of Science and Technology began coordinated science plans from 1974. The recent plans lay stress on envirnmental impact of the various developments and there is also importance attached to applications and use of the computers and their development. The department spends about Rs. 200 crores (1 crore=10 million) on mainly new thrusts and some unattached independent research establishments.

Estimated electronic production in billion rupees in the seventh five year plan period 1985-1990.

(From annual report of Department of Electronics)

Sector	Value
Components	56.2
Consumer Electronics	63.8
Communications	80.0
Broadcasting	7.5
Aerospace and Defence	23.2
Instrumentation and Industrial electronics	59.1
Computer and Office equipment	34.4
Total	324.2

A Department of Electronics was set up by the government in 1970 primarily to promote electronics industry and electronics based employment and exports in the country. It has set up public undertakings like the Electronics Trade and Technology Development Corporation, Computer Maintenance Corporation and a Semiconductor Colmplex. It is also engaging in Radar Systems Consultancy and production. Electronic packages are being made and delivered for meteorological, oceanographic and antarctica research. Antenna for community TV receivers are developed and manufactured. The department has pursued the manufacture of TV camera lenses, solid state microwave oscilloscopes, large scale integration, liquid crystal displays etc. and has entered into technoloy transfer agreements with sources of such know-how in many countries. A number of agencies like the Bharat Electronics Ltd. Electronics Corporation of India, Indian Telephone Industries, Bharat Heavy Electricals, Central Electronics Ltd. and certain Ordnance factories are engaged in the development and production of complex electronic equipment. Private sector is assisted in many ways in setting up and expanding electronic goods manufacture. India is exporting about Rs. 2 billion worth of electronic assemblies to electronic manufacturers and traders abroad in 1984 alone out of production worth Rs. 18.6 billion rupees. India is not yet self-suffcient in the manufacture of chips and microprocessors and large quantities are being imported for consumer goods industry providing employment to many people in the country and in the tax free manufacturing zones. The estimated electronic production in billion rupees in the seventh five year plan period (1985-1990) is given above from the report (1985) of Department of Electronics.

After the first world war, progress meant electrification, now it means use of electronics, computers and automation. The countryside is criss-crossed by power lines and communication links. Cities bristle with TV antennas. Giant pylons and communication aerials have changed the landscape. New energy resources are making villagers in the remotest corners and the adivasis conscious of electricity, electric light and progress. City children often have toys around computers on which they can play games. Government is encouraging investments by foreigners especially non-resident Indians in electronics and computer industries as such industries increase employment and are the decentralised skill intensive industries par excellence for the future.

6. Transnational industrial development

At the time of independence India had vary low production of crude and had to import almost all her growing requirements from abroad. Strenuous efforts to set up petro-chemical industry ended in many multi-nationals entering the Indian market through subsidiaries, licensees and joint ventures in cooperation with state or private enterprise, since only the multinationals had the necessary capital, equipment or know-how in this field. Invariably the agreements were such as tended to perpetuate technological colonialism. The units in India had their production, management and profits practically controlled from abroad. The Engineer India Limited was a correct step but in general it stayed for a long time as an ineffective figurehead for syphoning off royalties and know-how costs from the third world countries to the Western multinational principals. The petrochemical transnationals had close links with Western manufacturers of equipment, and with engineering consultants in their own countries. They took care that hardly any design work was automatically transferred to the Indian counterparts. The Indian equipment industries absorbed imported technology imperfectly, and often were blocked by outlandish material specifications and the guarantee conditions. India had dearth of technologists trained in engineering R&D and management. There were other constraints towards forward action like construction delays and inefficient planning and management. There would be high downtime often due to faulty inspection or maintenance of imported equipment. There were chronic power shortages, and poor quality of some Indian equipment and materials because of acceptance of lowest quotation and emphasis on paper work than on the merits of the transaction. An often-quoted example is the unsuccessful attempt at the development of longwal mining of coal in India while the same process has been quite well developed in Australia.

The power of the transanationals lies in the knowledge that they possess. In 1962 four largest American corporations controlled 61 per cent of all patents for bulk industrial cross-licensing and market sharing arrangements, especially for dyestuffs, chemicals and agrochemicals. The close nexus between industrial firms and engineering contractors block some self-help initiatives in the third world countries. This nexus ensured that the licensees have only partial access to all the segments of a technology. Basic know-how of chemistry, thermodynamics, reactor kinetics and basic process calculations were not considered essential parts of the transfer of tecnnology.

Compared to the achievements of Engineer India, the work of the R&D cell in the Fertilizer Corporation of India is regarded as better in performance. The preponderance of transnationals reflecting the early efforts of free India for industrialization has been the weakest link in India'a technical capabilities. The necessary industrial production could be brought about by using somewhat out-dated technology at great cost. The situation can improve only when the existing industry assists the R&D cells by generating design and process control data, for process improvement and modernization of these plants.

In the drug industry also, even though Indian industry has the capacity of making the bulk chemicals, the multinationals rely on the R & D for animal and clinical experiments to push their formulations and on the strength of their intensive sales drives and incentives to traders they get away with greater part of the profits. Indian pharmacopoeia can struggle by insisting on better clinical Indian R&D based on useful chemicals and simple formulations.

Often the imported plants and machinery are unnecessarily on too large a scale and thus the capital-output ratio is artificially too large. The plant should be on properly matched production steps. Our policy should be to make a proper choice and not diversify the plants for the same product so that our inventory on the national scale for spares and raw materials is kept low and capacity utilization is improved. The system of ancillary industries set-up for the purposes of large industries has given a great fillip to small scale industries. The quality control of raw materials and the finished components become the main bottlenecks if the small scale sector happens to be unsupported by community R&D assistance. Here some links between small scale industries, university researchers and research institutions have to become more active. A simple solution would be to expect all scientists and technologists to undertake private consultancy which must be appreciated by their employers including the government without inhibiting the same with too many rules and regulations.

6

SCIENCE AND PROSPERITY

1. Introduction

Science correlates with prosperity, but science will not immediately give production. Science has to be translated into new processes or new products through an innovation chain. Any society is prosperous when it produce more than enough for its own needs ; there is wherewithal for community services and good communications. An important ingredient for well-being of a society is internal and external security along with basic freedoms. Security also involves rule of law and an environment of peace and fair-play. Even before the advent of modern science there were oasis of prosperity for certain restricted geographical or class groups. More often the prosperous few belonged to an upper stata while the great mass of the people were either slaves or engaged in subsistence agricultural or craft labour or were born and bred into menial service of the upper classes. Modern science has produced new sources of energy and tools of production as well as new methods of management and use of information The cheap labour is no longer necessary. The machines can take over all hard labour. For wide-spread prosperity, distribution of goods or incomes must reach everyone. One way would be to accord free rations to cover the basic needs of food, shelter and clothing to all as is sometimes done to the members of a large work force or to the volunteers in security forces. In the absence of abundance of every kind and for ensuring individual freedom and compensation graded to abilities, the capitalist way is to assure to all work for income, and essential supplies. This is a superior way since individual talents can produce proportional returns. In the case of rental or royalty income on the national scale as for example for the oil rich countries, every one directly has a share in it. But for the developing countries where much more hard work by the population is required for increasing the national production, the best method is to provide work for all. However industrialisation with large factories and large state or private agricultural farms can produce greater production, no doubt, but may not automatically provide distribution of wealth. For reaching the entire population, society has to undertake further steps. Work could be provided by large scale nation-building tasks or development of infra-structure or by organising a host of small scale production units like handicrafts or by encouraging self-employment. Gandhian economics expects the rich owners of large industries or large farms to act as trustees on behalf of the common man and to syphon off profits for public utilities and charitable service institutions. In normal society committed to social justice, the distribution of incomes has to be organised independently of the inclination of rich 'trustees'. This is attempted by taxation alongwith incentives for capital formation and further investment as well as by offerring easy loans to all people for self-employment and lastly by undertaking public works of possible economic importance. Continuous expansion of extensive small scale industrial production and peasant proprietorships for intensive agriculture and animal husbandry assist in percolating income down to the masses. A minimum wage which is sufficient for staying above the poverty line defined by the circumstances of the economy, is usually fixed by law. The citizens could also be allowed to earn as much as they can by legitimate means. Unfortunately most developing countries have notions that allowing the same persons to do multiple jobs for increasing his or her income will rob someone else of a wholetime or a part time job. This prediliction in favour of false 'socialist' distribution of poverty is a hindrance to better living standards for all. It is the enterprise and motivation of individuals which will bring about prosperity in an emerging nation. The restrictive rules that exist in most developing countries against any employee using multiple skills are against prosperity. Increasing the output of work per person is the sure recipe for higher standards. Often one is paid for a specific job, but one could also be given a qualification pay for other abilities which could then be put to use on some occasion or the other. Qualification pay for officers is quite common in the armed forces.

Giant modern industries do not create new jobs commensurate with the investment, but such industries produce plenty of product for making it available cheaply to those that can afford. For prosperity there must be a mix of small scale production and expansion of services for wider distribution of incomes and large scale machine-based industries and industrial scale farming for breakthrough in production and material wealth. This calls for a mixed economy of both public and private sectors.

Science or modern knowledge is the beginning of the production process. An off-spring of science that now towers above it is engineering and a mix of science and engineering known as technology is equally important for production. Besides planning, financial resources, trained manpower, machines and raw materials etc. are necessary. Converting the products into national wealth requires sales and cultivation of markets and putting the products to human use. For the initial planning, one has to pinpoint a need or a projected need, and plan to meet it in a competitive manner by using efficient and economic methods of production often involving new processes and instruments which are results of sustained science, engineering and technology. The basic idea of the need and an attempt to meet the same in an original manner is termed innovation. Most industrial expansion is based on the innovative process. The innovation chain is generally accepted to involve cooperative endeavour of more than one person in intuition, science, technology, engineering, pilot plants, market survey, instrumentation, environmental impact analysis, systems study, sales, maintenance, safety etc., etc. One can guess that the effort spent in the innovative chain is about ten times that spent in the initial patentable creative contribution of scientists or engineers.

2. Investment in science and engineering

U.K. had made massive investment of money and effort in science after the last war. They found in the sixties that the industrial growth in certain other countries like West Germany with lower effort in basic subjects was better and this set them to analyse the relative contribution of science towards industrialisation. Prof. P.M.S. Blackett pointed out this importance of latter part of the chain to the Indian planners, but it would be misapplication to neglect investments in science. The investments in Science will not immediately lead to more industrialisation which will depend in the short run on investments in the latter part of the innovation chain. By not attending to all the links of the innovation chain and only increasing or lowering the investment in science will not help immediate industrialisation. In India there has been an urgent need to invest all along the chain and even the investment in basic science subjects is not commensurate with our needs of advancement. One must also bear in mind that scientific discoveries and inventions only give ideas for future products and a time-lag of ten to fifteen years is necessary to produce items for the users. Nuclear fission discovered in 1938 produced cheap power in 1950 in U.S.A. and in 1956 in India. The time elapsed was relatively small since considerable effort had gone in the study of nclear technology on account of defence needs. Progress in science involving new discoveries and new technologies takes quicker shape in universities and institutions devoted to fundamental science. In India after the impoverishment of the universities during the war and during the first decade or so after the war, attention has again been devoted to the educational system especially the higher education in sciences and social sciences.

There apparently is little interdepartmental planning in our universities. The students seem to worry only about passing the examinations which can perhaps also be done by insisting on lower standards and they are not so keen along with many of the teachers to improve the instruction and be abreast of the advances in the subjects of study. The semester system so necessary for better instruction in which the students are on notice for almost continuous examination through home work and weekly quiz, has been parodied in India. It has only amounted to the old type of examination to take place every six months rather than every two years. If there is proper course coordination and freedom of choice of subjects is given to students the efficiency of teaching will improve. The professional institutions like some of the institutes of technology or the Defence Institute of Armament Technology have begun this in earnest and the results and efficiency of output compared to input is materially increased. Besides engineers and technologists we need many other specialists in the innovation chain with basic knowledge of sciences. Many of the institutes of technology are attempting to give education in science and social science subjects upto arts degree standard in the first two years of the five year course. It would be in the interest of competitive efficiency if entry into the third year of technology courses or equivalent stage of other professional courses is also open to some selected graduates in science subjects from the universities. This will ensure better motivated students to displace some of the passengers in the degree classes. Recent trend is to scatter costly instruments in selected university departments or instrument centres with the hope that the instruments will be used by more than one department of a university or by many neighbouring institutions. This kind of cooperation and coordination can become a fact only if more funds are made available for research studies and when interdepartmental instruction becomes a fact for providing the necessary back-up experience.

New technologies rarely emerge from Indian universities unlike their counterparts in U.S.A or England because of the paucity of research support in the past and because of lack of faith and support from managements. Instrument development projects and funds must be available with most teaching and research departments. Part-time development work or pilot plant work should be available to science students so that they have a feel for technology development, and they also support themselves partially. The teachers supported by young minds will certainly produce new technologies as well as a real training in self-reliance.

There is also considerable misuse of 'planning' in the universities. The funds are alloted on project basis. Well designed projects can only be in the development of instruments or equipment and not for basic scientific research where well designed control points for the satisfaction of the financial and administrative authority do not exist in general. The funds for basic research should be disbursed on trust for long term to the leader of the group or to qualified and potentially productive individuals. The usual complaint however is that funds get only to the manipulators and glib talkers or to persons with leverage for unimportant studies for which the expected results depend on some change of parameters in well recognised experiments. Some research projects are mere duplication of developments abroad.

The environment of appreciation and encouragement so necessary for cretive work is rarely available in bureau-cratic funding and planning. University assistance to innovators and small scale industries should be freely available without any special liaison departments by the simple expedient of advertising private consultancy practice of university teachers and reseachers allowed under the usual government rules for private practice by government employees. The time spent for such assistance must be paid for by the clients at some flat rate. The consultancy work will provide some living problems for university teaching and research as well as introduce some students under the supervision of their teachers to solving practical problems. This may also inspire the universities to carry forward some applied basic science studies. It is also well known that creativity is increased in a creative individual if he is exposed to additional work not directly involved in his narrow specialization.

Every university must appreciate the value of continuing education for its teachers and its alumni and for others interested. The extension courses could also be arranged for the general public. There is hardly much being done for advanced continuing education or for general science education for the public or the politicians. The correspondence courses or the open university degrees are on a different footing since these are examination oriented, meant for employees who want to study for a degree at their own pace in their private time and these courses are no substitute for advanced courses of short duration say ten to thirty lectures distributed over a week-end or an entire month of evenings. The continuing education is required for scientists and technical people on account of new developments and new requirements of higher jobs that people get promoted into by age and length of useful employment. The continuing education can be arranged by the university departments in cooperation with employers of any viable group of scientists and engineers.

Our education system is saddled with an examination system which only hinders any modern training in problem solving or for research. The education is meant to prepare a student for a certain purpose and the examination must test the degree of preparedness of the student to meet that purpose. The test should be a feed-back for both the students as well as the teachers. The teachers must be free to improve the contents of their courses in order to benefit from these tests. The purpose of education is to enable students to take decisions, to solve problems, to reach and understand the source material of their subject. The judgement, the memory, the understanding and the logical faculty all have to be tested. For framing appropriate fresh test problems and allowing reference books and appropriate time to solve such problems, the teachers themselves have to work a lot and the absence of devoted work by both teachers and the students have made a mockery of the semester system copied from abroad. Non-teaching duties on honorary basis or on part-time basis should be assigned as far as possible to teachers and students to reduce dependence on or crowding by non-teaching staff.

The vice-chancellors should have the authority to transfer resources from within the university departments so that any budding technology or research break-throughs can be assisted and any non-productive lines almost terminated. The departments should be provided catalysts in the form of visiting faculty and older experienced teachers should be encouraged to write out lecture notes and textbooks. Only the best students should be admitted on the basis of their record or an entrance examination. Reservation of seats should be minimum say at a total of about ten per cent to certain nominees on the basis of economic or social backwardness but having adequate previous knowledge. Some additional seats may be created for nominees of neighbouring countries as a part of policy of South Asian and international coorporation. All the students in general should be totally supported by scholarships or campus employment.* The self-help of students during their education is the best guarantee for self-reliance after studies. The nominees for reserved seats or additional seats have to be given special coaching in the evenings and if the course results are much below average, a student should be relegated after every few months irrespective of whether he was accepted on merit initially or through reserved quota.

* Spicer Memorial College at Pune has followed this practice. but ironically their degrees, are not recognized in India, though the alumni do well in higher studies abroad.

3. Investment in applied science

A developed country prefers to farm out applied science projects to private or public research and development groups. In special fields where universities or production development groups in existing institutions are not found adequate, special institutions are speedily put together around suitable nuclei. Special R&D institutions are also built for military specialization not adequately covered by university researches or R&D work in private industries. In the United States some great institutions have existed for industry like the Bell Telephone laboratories or the RCA laboratories or the laboratories and test facilities of General Dynamics etc. Besides the natural preference for carrying out in-house development by industry, the system of using university professors as consultants besides other consultants is wide-spread. This automatically harnesses universities for applied research within their capability. This is about time to have simpler financial or travel rules for encouraging liaison between universities and industry.

When India embarked on rapid industrial development and self reliance, the university applied research was at a rather low level partially because no effort at all had existed there for the development of research instruments in the country. Course development in science and technology had also suffered because of the slavery to existing syllabus and lack of enterprise among the university teachers. The need for self reliance especially for defence was critical. The traditional suppliers of equipment had been the sources in U.K. and there was grave danger of supplies drying up especially when Indian foreign policy was non-aligned and the chief threat at that time was from Pakistan, a protege of U.K. and U.S.A. Besides purchasing armaments from all possible suppliers and working the elementary armament manufacturing capacity to the limit, there was an urgent need for mastering new fields of defence technology. In principle research projects of defence interest could be farmed out to the university departments but much could not be achieved in this way and a large number of defence research establishments had to be set up. In case some university professor did suggest a basic science project of possible interest to defence, the procedure for the grant of funds from defence was cumbersome and the interest would soon flag. The financial authorities desired the expected result to be exactly spelled out along with the programme of work and the date of completion. They had a notion that basic research would be progressed like a job of civil construction entrusted to a building contractor. The proper way to harness universities talents would be to select a university group or a suitabte specialist professor and support him financially for a longish period for a particular area of study. The defence authorities seem to have learnt the hard way and of late certain suitable departments of some teaching institutions are being liberally funded for applied basic research especially in radar, sonar, communications and rocketry. There is also an indirect gain of development of the infra-structure for applied research in the universities and engineering institutions.

The private and initially also the public sector was so intent on importing turnkey plants or the detailed know-how with usual restrictive clauses for the use of materials and instruments and specifications laid down by the principals, that there was hardly any creative initiative left worth the trouble for the local technical managers or the in-house R&D if any. For the slightest notion of improvement or modification of the raw materials or the process parameters, the Indian industry had to refer to their principals. Only the Soviet authorities sometimes went out of their way to guide the Indian managers to suitable Indian experts without harm to guarantee terms. Under such condititions, the setting up of applied research institutions in the country was like the setting up of higher education in King Arthur's England by Mark Twain's yankee. This was just a matter of faith that some day the laboratories will be useful to industry when the industry in India came of age. The users are now already keenly appreciative of the existence of the Atomic Energy Research Laboratories, Defence R&D Organization, and many other applied research institutions. Agricultural research was on a different footing, since its results were of interest to a multitude of farmers and the usefulness increased tremendously when appropriate extension services, communications and chemical inputs were expanded. So far as mechanical and chemical industry for agriculture is concerned, the purely Indian know-how is still very little in use, much more reliance is based on multi-nationals, but the Bhopal tragedy in Union Carbide factory has brought home to the people the slip-shod choice of agro-chemicals and maintenance of plant by the multinationals in developing countries.

India did act ahead of the times, but the results are now very pleasing, in establishing chains of research establishments which are now the key to self-confidence for future growth. Some of the work is related to the infra-structure like exploration, cataloging, meteorology, work-study, underwater acoustics, antenna design, quality control, Indian standards and national collections, remote sensing, Himalayan Geology, Oceanography, radio propagation, electrochemical processes, aeronautical research etc. etc. Many of these laboratories also helped in the maintenance of imported plants and now some of these are fully integrated with the needs of defence, energy production, oil refining, electronics, drugs and chemicals industries etc. Some of the important applied science and engineering institutions are—BARC, Central Fuel Research Institute, Central Mechanical Research Institute, Central Water and Power Research Institute, Defence Electronics Research Laboratories, Defence Institute of Physiology and Allied Sciences, Defence Materials and Stores R&D Establishment, Indian Institute of Petroleum, Institute of Petroleum Exploration, Instruments Unit of Department of Meteorology, National Aeronautical Laboratory, National Physical and Chemical Laboratories, Naval Chemical and Metallurgical Laboratory, Pasteur Research Institute, Physical Research Laboratory, R&D Department of the Bharat Electronics Limited, Railway Research and Designs Institute, Central Marine and Central Inland Fisheries Research Institutes and the National Institutes of Oceanography etc. etc. The annual expenditure on R&D work is around Rupees One thousand crores and is increasing @ 10 per cent per annum for government institutions. This effort does not cover current expansion of in-house research and development effort in the industries both public and private. A proper estimate is not possible since many units are only spending units for gadgets and for infructuous expenditure as the expenses are deductable from taxes.

The Private industry in West Germany financially supports 65 per cent of all civilian industrial research. This figure is about 45 per cent for France. The French Government has recently announced further tax deduction for investments in R&D. They have also a scheme for rotation of in dustrial researchers into government institutions for about a year after every few years, so that there is more interaction between industrial researchers and applied basic science groups. For best advantage there must be free mobility of scientists between academics, applied research and industrial research activities.

4. Production development

In the innovation chain, after a product or process has been identified from the accessible information banks, or from work of scientists and engineers in science laboratories, next important stage is to prove the process at a reasonable scale on a pilot plant and then to carry forward experimental production in the successful pilot plant or in some experimental production facility. The production development stage is the most effort consuming. An entire pilot plant may be wasted or an experimental production batch may not meet the specifications that are in view. There must be a cushion for such losses. The Indian patents and research results were often not sought by entrepreuners and industrialists mainly because the whole gamut of production development was yet to be carried out. Only now the industry is getting wise to reserving some capacity for experimental production and having seprate funds for production development. The National Research and Development Corporation also assists in pilot plant work by allowing a subsidy for products and processes for which the laboratory know-how is leased from them acting on behalf of various goverment and university laboratories. Where a well established industry is interested, the work of this stage is not difficult and the research laboratory that has got the know-how to offer can share considerable pilot-plant work as they sometimes have the appropriate scientific and engineering talents also. On this account most of the product or instrument oriented research establishments are now advised to associate an existing established industry or a factory of a related kind from the very start of the scientific research project or at least when reasonable prospects for the successful conclusion of the laboratory work is in sight. Production development in isolation might lead to disappointment if appropriate techno-economic survey does not exist, which will be the natural first job for the interested industry. After the pilot plant experiments, the manufacturing process, the required equipment, the raw materials and the product specifications can be written out.

Experimental production is necessary particularly for totally new products. This can be accomplished using the pilot plant itself or any other available manufacturing capacity by the enterpreuner, or as some batch production on the new plant if it is first assembled. The experimental production is necessary for conducting user trials or for developing the market by offering other purchase incentives. Sometimes a useful product does not succeed because of insuffiient sales promotion at the experimental production stage. Production development also often involves the large scale test facilities available with the public sector or certain government departments. Development efforts for Maruti used the facilities available at Defence Inspectorate of Vehicles.

5. Standards and quality control

Standards must be established for assurance of trade. Quality control ensure that the product is upto a given standard. Standards are arrived at jointly by the producers and the users. The users must get what is serviceable and the producers must not be required to produce what is not conveniently possible for the expected price range. Sometimes if the national standards have so far not been formulated, standards used by developed countries or international standards are adopted changing the specifications of raw materials where necessary and introducing corresponding limitations on the product. India very wisely set up the Indian Standards Institution in the initial stage of independent industrial development. A large number of British standards were adopted since considerable trade was initially with Britain. Sometimes large companies quote their own standards if the volume of their purchases or public acceptance of their products is on a large scale. Defence purchase in India often have their own standards, usually these are modified Indian National standards only regarding storage life or packaging conditions since defence supplies are not usually used immediately on purchase. Sometimes when the purchase is of stores that are short-lived like dry cells or certain chemical formulations, the defence indentors have to make special efforts to reduce the interval in the pipeline from the supplier to the actual user who may be in some inaccessible picket.

Quality control is essential at all stages of manufacture as well as periodically during storage and during use. Reliability means appropriate quality throughout the useful life. Quality and reliability have to be built into the product. by selecting appropriate component raw materials and methods of working and handling. The environment affects the performance and useful life and therefore the reliability. The manufacturer has to assure himself from field or user trials or laboratory modelling of the environment that the product has the necessary reliability and expected life. Drugs and antibiotics have a limited life in the pack since these deteriorate with time on account of low level chemical action that proceeds continuously. For structures, the role of environment for corrosion, loss of apperance, life of delicate moving parts etc are important. Air conditioning or special atmospheres in packaging and in use are specified. Standards include as basis the following : composition, performance, use, design, finish and packaging, and useful life both in storage as well as in operation.

6. Packaging, sales and maintenance

Packaging must assure the same quality at the user end what has been observed in the inspection room at the factory. Packaging and storage of the equipment when idle or in transit must be such that reliability is unaffected. The home market is so vast in India that any proper packing for Indian destinations would be good for similar places in the world. India has all the variations of climate. European manufactures often run exposure or field ranges in tropical climates so that they can infer proper packing and performance specifications. Within India, costs could be rationalised by having different packaging requirements for different destinations e.g. the tropical land mass or the cold Himalayan regions.

Sometimes imported equipment costing lakhs of rupees has been wasted because the packing was not properly specified and they sent the equipment in ordinary trade packing which limits the life of the packed delicate equipment to only fourteen days and shipping to India from abroad as well as clearing the equipment at the Indian ports often took few months.

Corrugated cardboard packing is fairly good, provided the pack is not exposed to rain outdoors. The standards for packaging exist for packing materials as well as its design. There is an

Indian Institute of Packaging to which problems could be referred for advice. There are many inexpensive wraps to safeguard costly leather, glass, steel and electronics equipment or costly seeds against fungal attack or ravages of corrosion or biological deterioration during storage. Most countries still do not have fungal resistant wraps that will ensure quite cheaply the fungal-proofness in hot and humid climates, partly because they are not continuously faced with the problem. Stores manufactured in India have this advantage that these can easily be wrapped satisfactorily. The national Research Council in Czechoslovakia has done considerable work on the modelling of climates and the mathematical design calculations for packaging. The Defence Research Laboratory for Materials have carried out many important studies in surface treatment of materials and in the design of suitable protective wraps. Some of their products are not yet in common use because of indifferent market development by them. The costly glass parts and microscope slides so commonly used in medical research, are often seen to be pitted from fungal attack, but are wrapped in costly decorative plastic films which give no real protection. Special packaging requirements exist for stores that have to be dropped by parachute or which suffer much vibrations and jolts during transit. To avoid wastage, a developing country must give attention to specialised packaging, storage stability and reliable performance.

Marketing of the product is a serious rung in the ladder of innovation. It is successful sales that support production and make a success of the innovation. In many large industries it is the marketing manager who is often promoted to the position of the general manager. For increased production of many new products, the customers have to be convinced of the need to buy the new product through advertisement, demonstration or the usual sales promotion gimmicks. The recent steps for easy loans to entrepreuners and towards self employment have created a market for certain articles. The general level of increased prosperity also has increased the demand for all kinds of products. Still many instruments, electronic gadgets, and sophisticated machinery are imported. There is room for import substitution and also for the Indian made quality goods at competetive prices particularly for the export market.

A product is always more popular and enjoys better market, if trained operators and adequate after-sales service are available. Availability of genuine spare-parts also helps. Many large industries help the growth of licenced production of spares and accessories. There is the scandal of costly instruments lying idle in hospitals or industrial inspection rooms for want of properly trained technicians who could maintain the equipment in trouble-free condition. Recently national and regional instrumentation centres have been established so that many users could resort to these for their occasional requirements of costly equipment or use the repair facility created there for their own equipment. The facility can be easily expanded by having also electronics and instrumentation experts who could routinely visit desirous industries for checking their equipment on a kind of equipment audit visit. A defective instrument not recognized as such can be a serious hazard in a medical institution for example. Easier maintence is also a design parameter. For most equipment, modular structure with easily replaced modules is recommended, One must in principle have regular maintenance of all equipment as they do for aircraft where intervals for checking, lubrication, minor and major overhauls are laid down in detail. In India there is no philosophy of early discard and the environmental conditions are rather severe, therefore, one can say with pride that maintenance and repair are well attended to here. Cars for example have useful life of decades. Reliability engineering is also carried out during design, quality control and inspection procedures. India is still lagging in reliability engineering only because long-lived reliable electronic components and suitable alloys with superior creep and fatigue properties have to be imported. The facilities for creep testing are now being created to match the growth of alloy production. Facilities already exist in many laboratories for fatigue testing against vibrations under stress or for testing of springs of all kinds. Most micro-electronics is in sealed units embedded in suitable plastics or elastomers, and redundancy is employed for components or assemblies towards better reliability.

7. Performance of the Indian Economy

From 1947 to 1985. the population of India had arisen from 300 million to more than double, the agricultural and industrial production had increased fourfold. Since India became self-sufficient in food, the prosperity (product per person) has risen at roughly the rate of 2% per annum, and is rising at a higher rate now. The imports and exports have arisen ten-fold. The industrial work force is three times what we started with. About 11% of all workers are now engaged in industry. To make a real impact on the purchasing power, the industrial work force should increase to about 30% of the total work force and the increase in agricultural production has to be maintained by inducting better agricultural technology and not allowing or forcing more people to join subsistence farming since the size of farms already is very small. The work force in the infra-structure of education, information, health and administration can increase considerably from the present 10% of the entire work force. The efficiency of all workers is rather low. The output per worker in industry is only about double that of the average worker in agriculture. The efficiency and work output of an industrial worker should be ten times that of an agricultural worker for employing him at about double the wages in order to compensate for the cramped conditions of work and its repetitive nature. This would mean better management of industries and more automation and multiple skills of the workers. In the table below the distribution of workers in various occupations is given for 1981.

Occupation	Total Number (in thousands)
Cultivators	90,000
Agricultural labourers	53,000
Manufacturing including cottage industries	11,500
Construction	2,000
Trade, transport and communications	7,000
Total	163,500

The unemployed job seekers increase each year at the rate of two million, requiring job expansion of about 4% so that the increase in work force balances the wastage. It is partly for this desirable increase in work force that the output-efficiency per worker is not particularly striven for and as a result income per worker is likely to remain relatively low. We have to increase the number of jobs, the production per job, the services, the home market as well as exports. For such expansion, the constraints of materials and energy resources can be overcome only through science, technology and use of machines and robotics.

The comparative gains registered by the public sector are relatively low compared to equal investment in the private sector. This is on account of non-commercial pricing in the public sector and unaccounted utilization of public facilities and indifference often to social impact by the private sector. There is also scope for managing the public sector for legitimate profit and charging the private sector for public facilities and social action as may become necessary. Often the prices charged from the customers are disproportionate to the legitimate expenses in the private sector. In a protected market like ours and when wages are much lower in India than in foreign countries, the prices should be lower and we should have much larger share of the export market. This is partly not happening because of the cost-inefficiency of the private sector. One could watch the price structure in various manufactures and bring to light the mal-practises of managements that artificially bloat the expenditure in our private sector while no one is being paid by international standards and it is alleged that the management and the proprie-tors get salaries which are less than what is paid even to the public sector counterparts. The secret lies in the malpractices, the black money, under-invoicing etc. for the owners on a grand scale. If the investments are properly insured and enter-preuners can draw adequate credit, there is no reason for extraordinary hoarding of unearned wealth by the nabobs of the private sector.

The mismatch between education and employment needs correction. The government is now seriously considering modi-fications in the education system. Rural schemes of training for self employment are gathering momentum. Technical training is likely to be organised on the basis of job requirements and con-tinuous education as well as conversion training will become important ingredients of adult education.

The changing pattern of consumption expenditure shows

increasing viability and prosperity in an Indian family. Ten years ago, the expenditure on consumable durables was 0.34% but later in 1982, this rose to 5%. The astronomical rise of imports and exports point to the health and aspirations of the Indian Society. India's policy of liberally responding to the development needs of the LDCs' through the UN agencies, through the Colombo plan, and on direct government to government basis indicates an awareness of her international role of being a change agent for peace and progress of the world. The South Asian Regional Cooperation is likely to be an important inter-government programme in South Asia.

India has been pragmatic in the organization of its production.

The private sector including the land owned by tillers, cooperative sector especially in the village industries and distribution of agricultural inputs and rural enterprises based on handlooms, cattle, sugarcane etc,. public sector, state enterprises, foreign subsidiaries, multinationals, joint ventures of various kinds, all have their proper niche. The current winds of competition and efficient service may show up certain arrangements as superior or even some of the inefficient or over-expensive managements may have to cease functioning or seek salvation in taking shelter in better run systems.

The planned use of 200 deep sea fishing trawlers by the end of 1990, will make it necessary for popularisation of marine fish as food item. The Indian planners see a rise in the export of engineering goods, chemicals, gems, leather, garments, marine products by 5.4% per annum in real terms. The total outlay in the 7th five year plan is likely to exceed Rs. 200 thousand crores. The share capital dividends declared in 1985 amount to 12 to 13% per annum and the price index has been rising at the rate of about 8%, which shows the healthy state of the economy. There has been a sustained growth rate at fixed prices of about 5% and it is expected to be higher in future. The population increase has also indicated a definite drop.

The Ministry of Industry has announced recently that it is planning to free as many areas as possible from license controls. The Bureau of Public Enterprises has advised the public sector to encourage more ancillary industries both upstream and downstream for cheaper products so that there is more production.

The policy of dual quality for satisfying compulsory levies at reduced rate, for the vulnerable section among customers, has to be such as to keep the sugar, paper and textile industries competitive. This is sought by government subsidies, allowing much larger price for the open market and special incentives for export etc. However, there is considerable scope for price reduction through technology change, efficiency improvement and scrutiny of unwarranted expenditure by the managements. The state owned semi-conductors Ltd. at Chandigarh will soon be producing micro-electronics components and micro processors for CLASS (Computer Literacy and Study in Schools), including rural educational programmes) along with other uses. . . . The green revolution is now in its second phase spreading into the States of Bihar, M.P. Orissa, U.P. and West Bengal.

India is now exporting veterinary preparations, medical equipment and instruments to USSR and the overall figure of exports to USSR amounts to Rs. 4,000 crores per annum which means an increase of 20% over the previous year, Similar rise has been in the overall figure for the entire world. India also exports consultancy and technical services particularly in the area of railways and communication, education and health. A greater emphasis is being placed on self-sufficiency in edible oils and the export of perfumery oils and chemical intermediates.

The economic performance is not fully represented by the published statistical data. The whole scene is bedevilled by the black money or the so-called parallel economy. A considerable part of the income stays hidden for avoiding government taxes. Apart from such inome with the traders and shopkeepers, there is considerable undeclared income accruing to professionals, landlords and factory owners and to downright criminals like smugglers and corrupt contractors and officials. There are also phoney charities, phoney business losses and phoney business expenses including writeoffs of expenditure on R&D never actually carried out etc. etc. An estimate is that there is the generation per annum of black money amounting to Rs. 1300 crores. This vast sum is usually spent in showy opulence, weddings and speculation in precious metals and real estate. The enormous expenditure on consumables causes more inflation, and supports black market and smuggling etc. Of the same nature as black money is the industrial cxtravagance by corrupt banking officials in misusing the various financing schemes by granting loans that have to be writtcn off. Still the insurance could allow the writing of some loans where the inability to refund happens due to reasons not related to the inefficiency or misuse by the entreprenuers.

India is in the forefront of the international movement for a new economic order. A review of the functioning of the international banking and trading practices has become necessary in the interest of an equitable chance of development for most of the developing world, and therefore in the larger interest of the developed countries too. U.S.A. desires a review in the reverse direction since its own products are threatened in the domestic market by imports. But such fears are universal and some competition must be experienced by all countries that desire also to export. The remedy lies perhaps somewhat in the reduction of the highly inflated value of the dollar. The GATT provisions must also be liberalised making special allowances for countries faced with insurmountable difficulties in view of fewer mutual trade openings for them. It is quite possible for the world to hammer out broadly acceptable changes. The straws in the wind are indicative of success in the expected negotiations if approached in an enlightened manner for the greatest good of the greatest number without disproportionate sacrifices by others. A democratic consensus would emerge, we believe.

7

SOCIAL SCENE OF THE MID-EIGHTIES

1. Folk culture

As you sow, so shall you reap is ingrained in the Indian folk culture. Belief in transmigration of the souls is universal. An ordinary Indian has come to terms with both reason as well as faith. Faith is only a way of self assurance irrespective of reasoned expectations and reason can never give definite answers since all the data including the data from previous births is never there. The acute and widespread hidden hold of blind faith and magic still peep from happenings reported in the press from odd places. How recently there was a throng of thirty thousand villagers egging on and thirsting to see a widow burn herself on her dead husband's funeral pyre in Rajasthan and how the crime was avoided by an appeal to their blind faith that the pyre must get lit by supernatural means which did not happen. One hears sometimes the gruesome murder of a child victim for the ritual propitiation of the god of plentry, but the culprit is invariabte brought to book and the public applauds the punishment. One can go around a village and rarely notice charms tied around the limbs or the waist of a child which was a common sight fifty years ago. In old times most children, Hindu or Muslim had such a magic thread worn at the waist, being the relic of old fire worhip now found only among the handful of Parsis in India. Most Hindus were put through a ritual of being twice born by the sacred thread ceremony and they wore this sacred thread on the shoulder. Few people carry such Hindu symbols now. People seem to have lost the inclination for personal rituals of their faith, but they still perform social rituals at the time of births, weddings and deaths. Society allows abbreviation and curtailment of ceremonies. Folk festivals and religious fairs as well as crowds for the glimpse of gurus or god-men are popular. In general the common man is religious as well as very pragmatic, desirous of quick return from any observance or religious effort. The fairs offer them elevation of soul, entertainment and trade. The congregations provide discourses where attendance itself is considered meritorious and these also constitute social events.

Now-a-days the first recourse in the event of sickness is to the home-remedies and then to modern medicine if accessible or to other systems of medicine including homeopathy. When totally disappointed, the poor as well as the rich try faith cures by knocking at the doors of holy men or their tombs and of shrines. Lastly even the magicians and witch-doctors are tried. There are always some stray witch-doctors in backward areas who have widespread fame for particular cures. The schools, the educated village level workers, retired soldiers, government radio and TV, cinema and rural drama all have combined to spread awareness of modern science and use of facts and information based on real happenings. The technology based miracles are part now of every day life in most societies.

The struggle for existence for at least half the population is very severe. Cramped and unhygienic conditions abound around the life of unemployed, agricultural labourers and city slum dwellers. The common man however is very much cultured if by culture one means the primary concern for the welfare and happiness of others. In fact on this touchstone the poor of India will be found more cultured than the rich of any place. This can be seen by any stranger visiting some village or from the charitable instinct of a slum dweller who spares a morsel from his spartan meal for the stray dog or the likely bird. They will gladly give up their own work or leisure to be helpful to a total stranger, unlike the boorish bureaucrats who will not be civil to even their masters the common people. Thieving and cheating except by get-rich quick shop-keepers here and there is most uncommon. Newspapers often have stories of restoration of lost articles by cabmen, vendors and shop assistants. It is the God-fearing culture of the common man that allowed a handful of foreigners to rule over them and inspired rebellion only when saintly leaders like Guru Gobind Singh or Mahatma Gandhi could lead them.

2. Gangsters and hoodlums

A goonda is often a notorious character of the locality who believes in bullying and violence for his own benefit or the benefit of his chosen patron usually a politician, a police-man or a rich man of dubious means. (Would not dictators be goondas under this definition ?) Most people humour the goondas or tolerate them when the civic or state authorities are weak. Dadas (a variety of hoodlums) are slightly more acceptable as they may not personally commit crimes and be only intermediaries between the politicians and the anti-social elements. Both the goondas and the dadas are bullies. The police very often tolerate them since known goondas are regarded as helpful in solving crime in their recognised areas. It is the goondaism (or gangsterism) backed by corrupt and jingoistic politicians and desperate parties which is very harmful. It is the goondas that act as agent provocateurs for communal and other kinds of violent agitations and disturbances.

Mahatma Gandhi saw wide-spread disaffection and used as well as invented various modes of protest like strikes, hunger-strikes, picketing, law breaking, processions etc. Once India became free and self-governing under a democratic constitution, there should have been no more need for vociferous and tumultuous protests. But there are some shortcomings in the practice of decision making by brute majority. Slowly we are learning the merits of consensus for controversial matters. Many times minority views have been heard only after agitations and protests that have led to rioting providing a field day to the political goondas. The grievances do not reach the powers also because most political organisations are not rooted in the mass of the people. Most of the better educated people have been in government service or look to government favours. The political organizations are often paper organizations created by professional politicians, with state, city and block satraps appointed by a central coterie. It is partly due to such conditions that legitimate feed-back is not available as for the state governments populous decision to reserve seats in educational and professional colleges for all kinds of backward classes with an eye on the next election or to make scheduled caste reservations even for promotions in government employment. When such decisions are taken without considering the harm accruing to the affected group of qualified youngsters or when regional riders are placed on economic assistance by state, many integrationists are genuinely concerned and protests lead to bandhs, non-violent agitations and later to rioting and attack on public property or on innocent people belonging to different communal or religious labels. Same kind of disturbances followed the idealistic total revolution floated by Shri Jai Prakash Narain and it is the goondas who soon following the spoken or unspoken ideas of the politicians egg on mobs to take to violence and loot. This happened also in the anti-Sikh pogroms which had a couple of days' sway in the major cities of North India after the assassination of Mrs. Gandhi. It is also the so-called moderates among Sikh politicians who stoke the fires of discontent leading to terrorist attacks by extremists that have held the Punjab Society at pistol point now for three years. Mrs. Indira Gandhi was catapulted into a second term of office on the basis of machinations of her younger son who had harnessed the energies of many goondas and dadas who demonstrated how her charisma could incidentally be exploited by unscrupulous people for self aggrendisement. The present government of Rajiv Gandhi is very much aware of the entrenched position of such unscrupulous people in the government and is exerting to get rid of these elements.

For the first few decades the democracy was functioning in a strange feudal manner. Whole castes and religious minority groups voted enblock for the candidate favoured by the local chief who was often himself never an elected head of the group. Recently it appears that people have started making personal decisions about the vote and fooled even the goondas and dadas. We still have instances of nexus between politicians and undesirable elements at the time of elections. There are instances of intimidation and booth capturing especially in U.P. and Bihar. In Rajasthan, the killing by a trigger happy police officer of a sitting MLA and a candidate for elections point to the same malaise. Sometimes political pessimism even in a democaracy, can lead to terrorism. This also reflects the distance of authority from feelings of people or misunderstanding by minority groups of the overall political goals of the nation. The problems become accentuated when there is obvious symbiotic relationship between the politicians and goondas or terrorists who provide the muscle power in exchange for protection. Such a situation converts certain police units into ones that hunt with the hounds and run with the hares.

The isolation of goondas from centres of authority is an uphill task begun recently in the country. A scientific attitude among the people in favour of fair play and equal rights of all will be against goondaism and violence. Such an attitude will ferret out the social and political conditions and constraints that seem to encourage goondaism and extra judicial centres of power that impinge on human rights of peaceful citizens and then suggest ways and means to improve these.

3. Secularism

For the last hundred years or so the weeds of communalism and parochialism were diligently nourised in India. The harvest was in the partition of India and continued misery of populations in many cities of India now notorious for communal riots, and genocidal tendencies in countries in the neighbourhood of India where also the poisonous weed has flourished even stronger after the independence of those countries. Bangladesh after her independence has re-embraced secularism but has not been able to avert military take-over.

Hinduism and various religions having roots in Hinduism like Budhism, Jainism, and Sikhism and other religions as practiced in India have basically a secular outlook. They recognise spirituality in all forms of faith and worship. The secularist dictum is 'Truth is one but it is expressed in many different ways.'

Comparative religion, pragmatism and humanism are regarded as the result of scientific attitude to religion. Humanism is in fact the literal translation of the Hindu word for religion. This indirectly confirms that Hindus had a scientific approach to religion. Comparative religion compares and contrasts various religions and points out basic similarities in all religions explaining various mythologies in terms of respective social needs and different childish explanations of mysterious observations. The analytical approach subtracts from the religion, the wonder and the sublime flights of fancy for harmony with inferred reality. Secularism is religion plus ; besides a soft corner for one's own beliefs, it requires equal respect and acceptance of co-existence of other religions. All religious people who aspire also to be cultured have no other option but to be secular in outlook. Jinnah struggled with success for Pakistan (a home-land for Muslims of India) but he was fundamentlly secular-minded person desiring other beliefs to have an honourable existence in Pakistan which cannot be said about his successors and usurpers in that country. On the whole, the people of India are reverting to their ancient humanism. The secular outlook, the principles of coexistence and non-alignment as well as feeling of concern for the independence of other peoples and their human rights are natural results of their age-old belief in humanism and their belief that the entire human race is but a single family.

Sikhism has been an intensely secular and humanist religion born of the devotional philosophies prevalent in India from the interaction of divergent faiths entering India. But the seeds of sparatism have flourished in the expatriate Sikhs especially those who left India before participating in the new reconstruction of the Hindu spirit anchored in secularism. Nexus between politicians and goondas in the country has also stoked the fires of communalism on flimsy pretexts or no basis excepting political aggrandizement of so-called leaders at the cost of the progress of the entire country.

Science has given most convincing explanation of natural phenomena and the astronomical observations or Earth's history and evolution. Many religious books were obviously propagating wrong concepts in these matters and modern man has to distinguish between the grain and the chaff in this kind of heritage. A truly religious mind can do so as he has his convictions also about science and secularism. Science is the true weapon for killing superstition including the addiction to astrology which happens to be worldwide. No one need quarrel with astrology as a mere pastime or as a study in the validation of certain intuitive knowledge of future events. Only when one tries to influence future events from phoney prescience, superstitious subservience to cheats starts. Astrology has very cleverly clothed itself in the garb of pseudo-scientific jargon of variables, synergism, probability, and recorded verifications whereas there can be no connection whatsoever between planets and human beings. India also like most ancient cultures has been steeped in the belief in astrology and to her misfortune has suffered historical defeats because of blind adherence of her rulers to astrology. Most of astrology is in fact based on intelligent or intuitive guesses, climate, heredity, social pressures, psychological readings and suggestions etc. The fuzziness in thinking and speech as well as fuzziness in memory and expectations chalk up sometimes an apparent success, but any plans depending on futures based on astrology can only harm people. Science has found no basis for astrology and its predictions could as well be made by charltans and chance machines. All over the world daily and weekly horoscopes for people are published in magazines. India has the distinction that certain popular magazines that used to publish such trash, no longer do so. The crutch of astrology also becomes desirable for gamblers. Gambling has been a national weakness in our country just like the British love of betting. Races of all kinds and betting on cricket, wrestling or flights of pigeons and cockfights have been common. A secular India is not puritan and there is no legal bar on such addictions. There is however no casino functioning in India anywhere. Prohibition was tried in most of India and enforcement became too prohibitive and soon the policy seemed to have nagative results. Drinking is permitted in private. Often there are deaths from indulging in drinking unhealthy brew prepared by unlicenced stills. India has licensed certain lotteries run by states or ostentatiously for humanitarian cause. Though some people do get lottery prizes yet lottery is essentially a punishment for the general public and a source of corruption for many people connected with the operation often fraudulent of such lotteries and quicker the evil is exorcised, the better it would be for the poor man. Sikhism bans tobacco, Hindus and Jains are vegetarians by preference though most people take fish. Muslims think it unclean to eat pork and Hindus think it sinful to eat beef. In secularism the non-believer does not infringe the taboo of the believer in any ostentatious manner so that there is no disrespect to neighbour's feelings.

A secular outlook looks askance at all kinds of discrimination. A secularist accepts the path of piety and right living as spelled out by various religions. Best secularist of this type has been Ramakrishna of Bengal and his disciple Vivekananda established the Ramakrishna mission which is widely credited with spreading the gospel of humanism and secularism. In free India once again the people have begun celabrating jointly the religious and seasonal festivals as they used to do before the poison of separatism was injected into their social life which ultimately led to migrations during the partition. Secular India has given up all kinds of legal or social discrimination, excepting some discrimination in the matter of education and jobs in favour of depressed classes of old. Logic demands removal of all discrimination but for the provision of special educational effort for economically backward families and groups. Merit, and experience must alone govern selection for jobs. Merit scholarships should be distinct from merit-cum-means scholarships so that merit scholarships are actually awarded as incentives to bright students irrespective of their coming from better-off families. One must repeat that once equal opportunities in education exist and weaker sections are afforded special coaching, the employment should be open only to merit.

We have obvious discrimination in favour of minorities in the matter of higher jobs. For high level jobs, apart from merit and experience the personal equation with the chief becomes equally important. As secularism and democracy strike deep roots, the feeling of being discriminated for or against will slowly dwindle. A minority in danger is a usual slogan of petty politicians to grind their onw axe. The hue and cry of certain Sikh spokesmen is also of the same type. Some of their 'intellectuals' have even misinterpreted their own scriptures to cut away their genuine links with the minority community of the Punjab whom they aspire to exploit. Secularism must assert to expose such theologians who play with the unity in India's diversity.

Many scholars, journals and media are widely conducting non-political discussions on themes of secularism and development. Discussion groups under the leadership of capable intellectuals are welcome for the spread of secular and scientific thinking. Some of the religious places of worship, libraries and political parties as well as humanitarian groups do and must sponser such discussions. A brief secular prayer for the prosperity of United India could be routine from all places of worship.

4. Population and essential needs

The degree of satisfaction in economic terms is given by the quotient of income by needs. The terrorists of the Punjab, or Manipur or the regionalists of Bombay or Hyderabad feel that short cut to prosperity is to throw out non-conformists and appropriate their properties and opportunities. The same was tried by the Nazis regarding the Jews and Sri Lankans were trying against Tamils. There have been genocides in the past and the pure have not flourished as a result. True wealth is in the productive ability of populations and not in passive property. Unless agricultural or industrial production can be increased, prosperity will remain will-of-the-wisp. By violence and plunder the production skills diminish. Before the advent of science and technology, there were limitations to economic production but these constraints are not important any more. Fertilizers can now be manufactured from coal and air. Energy is produced by hydroelectricity, nuclear fission and from sun's rays etc. Minerals can now be mined from the ocean bottom. Income per capita will also depend on the growth of population. With peace, population is increasing. India has doubled her population after independence. The new emphasis all over the world for control of population is indeed welcome. The rate of increase of population has materially decreased in the last decade. In Hindu mythology, wars and natural calamities were a dispensation for reducing population. Now deliberate family planning can bring this about. Incentives for small families and dis-incentives for large families are achieving the objective of reduction in population. The expansion of human horizons, and preference by certain cultures for the celib-ate life also limit population. The birth control pills and such measures are somewhat experimental in nature and their abuse could have subsequent health problems or lead to unacceptable proportion of malformed babies. Self-control or surgical interference by vasectomy or tubectomy are more trustworthy. In India it is expected that the population will stabilize in about fifty years at double the present figure and then it might slowly decrease. Greater efforts are required if the maximum population is to be restricted to stabilize at a lower figure within twenty years.

As suggested in the beginning of the section, satisfaction might increase also by reducing the needs. This was the basis for the philosophy of non-possession. Great Indians like the Buddha, the Jain ascetics, Muslim divines, Kabir or many wandering sanyasis were firm believers of non-possession and simple living. India of the future must unlearn some of the consumer culture that has been imbibed from U.S.A. The crisis in the Punjab is not due to fall of GNP per capita but due to soaring expectations and greed for more good things of life. For peaceful progress, every effort should be made to spread the merits of a simple life since inspite of science and technology the consumption standard of U.S.A. will not be reached in the developing countries for a long time. Why not then approach increase in well-being by emphasis on simplicity as was taught by Gandhi and so many others. Simple life does not mean fashionable wear of kurta or khadi., but it also means pleasure in simple food, simple clothing and simple and clean living quarters and simple entertaining. The politicians and journalists and other influential persons should desist from public adulation a la Khushwant Singh of liquor, loose living or participation in showy weddings and parties in five-star hotels. Our new set of values regarding consumption at least for next hundred years should continue to be built on the time-tested values which have special significance for the whole world in dire want. Wandering religious individuals should be assured of free food and shelter by town charities since such facilities are less supported now by individual charity. The sadhus and the like can then perhaps act as change agents for better morals, philosophical discussions and respect for the simple life. The greater charge on society is to assure satisfaction of the bare essential needs that of work and as a consequence, food, shelter and clothing. Even today, a large percentage of our people are living below the poverty line i.e. their share of essentials is less than the bare minimum. It is criminal to indulge in consumerism when so many have neither shelter nor clothing nor provision for the next meal. A minor cold wave causes numerous exposure deaths in our conntry. Some-times ten persons are crowded in a single room in a slum. So many live on the pavements in large cities. Socialism as well as enlightened capitalism want everyone's needs to be met. Gandhi also hoped to wipe away the tears in every eye. In the absence of work for all for food or for wages, schemes of dole for the unemployed, free education and free mid-day meals for children, cheaper or free distribution of cloth to weaker sections, easy loans for self employment are excellent steps. Everyone should be taught at least one handicraft to enable him to earn a little atleast. The example of the emperor Aurangzeb who darned prayer caps for earning his meals must be remembered with pride and it is something to be emulated by all.

Science and Technology have great deal to contribute to self-help for a simple life. Handicrafts for one's idle hours can be made more efficient resultwise by simple gadgets and inventions, and by harnessing of easily available source of energy like power from water or winds, bio-gas or sunshine. If scientists and engineers devote some attention to appropriate and rural technologies, the results will be literally extensive. The direction to the economy should be such as to distinguish between necessities and superfluous consumer articles. The necessities of modern life like watches, paper, bicycles, stoves, plastic or earthenware, lamps, books, fertilizer, cement, sugar, electrical machinery, fans, etc should even be imported so that market competition reduces the price and improves quality. The non-essential consumer articles like cars, scooters, petrol, fancy cloth, carpets, gems. gold and silver ornaments, kitchen gadgets, decoration pieces etc. etc. should be taxed heavily for the internal market but supported handsomely for the export market so that quality is improved and valuable foreign exchange can be earned and the consumerism is curtailed in the country. There should never be a premium on inefficient production by sheltring the home market or over much price support for exports. We may observe here that the toy industry of India is competing well both in the home as well as in the foreign markets. Same should happen regarding the most important modern manufactures of electronic goods and instruments.

There is shortage of food protein, and the standard re-cipe is to suggest expansion of marine fishing which is now around the corner and we must start development of the market for fish preparations now and also prepare refrigerated transportation where necessary. At present the Indian marine catch is only 2 million tons while it can be increased to 10 millions tons. The catch above the requirements of the domestic and export markets for food, can be used for the production of oil and fertilizer or for animal feed. There has also been a tremendous development in the inland pisciculture. India is now producing about $2\frac{1}{2}$ million tons of fresh water fish and the potential exists to double this amount by 2000 A.D. Production of feed grains and cereals is expected to keep pace with the requirements. Much more effort has yet to go in for milk production and distribution and for sheep farming for meat and wool. The progress is continuing.

Mahatma Gandhi demonstrated the significant contribution of self-help through the spinning wheel to India's emancipation. The spinning wheel in village homes can be perhaps replaced by home size spinning and weaving machines utilizing village electrification. There should be a scope for better household industrial machines of various kinds for cooperative production. There is scope for architectural planning of cheap housing and replacing tenements that create slums by more healthy group housing for labour. Community kitchens* as experimented by Pune professors and family barracks around the community kitchens should be tried in large cities or by resourceful firms for their labour force. The same design could also be recommended for retired or senior citizens who can also be provided with congenial work and recreation sheds in the neighbourhood. Designing of family based communal living, each individual being free to pursue his independent work with communal common services of most kind, should not be too much for achieving by our scientists and social workers.

Lack of work opportunities afflicts our villages which are sending an unending stream of manual labourers without any training or preparation for crowding in the slums of large cities. Efforts must be made to decentralise the industries away from large cities and to spread machine assisted handicrafts e.g. pottery and textiles in the villages.

5. Posttion of women

Sudden flare-up in the publicity of dowry deaths has highlighted the plight of Indian women at least belonging to the middle

* Indira Community Kitchens : For details contact Prof. P.V. Sukhatme, Professor of Biometry. Maharashtra Association for the Cultivation of Science, Law College Road, Pune 411007. About 2000 lunchens are sold @ Rs. 2/- per packet.

class. The presence of some highly gifted women in the highest ranks of the land gives a false sense of security with respect to the average status of the women. The sexual inequality has a built-in plight for most women after marriage. In order to improve their lot the women themselves have to be educated to improve the lot of the newly wedded bride into a family since major ill treatment is received from the women members of the family, who also manage to estrange the bridegroom from the new bride. Partly the basic cause is the economic slavery of women and the older women members feel their share of the family holding going down because of the fresh entrant. It is also the mothers who in general meet second class treatment to their own girl children since they are supposed to take away sooner or later a portion of the family wealth into another family. Recently a women's group marched on foot from Rajasthan to Delhi and reported that women's needs were totally ignored in the villages along the way. The women still suffer in a male chauvinistic society.

Legally the women in India have every equality with men. At the time of marriage any gifts or dowry given by the girl's parents or others are legally the personal property of the girl, who in actual life hears about these gifts when these are termed wholly inadequate for the high self-image of the husband's family. The married girl also has the legal right to the share equal to that of the brother in her father's property. This provision perhaps needs more elaboration but at present unfortunately it is often ignored or circumvented, as most parents disinherit the daughter through will or obtain her disinterestedness by cajolling her consent. The incogruity in the provision rests on the fact that the daughter has no social or legal responsibility after her marriage in the maintenance or looking after her parents, whereas the brother has to accept such a social responsibility, and the brother often has a joint family with the father after the sister is married away. In case the married daughter is earning, her earnings go to enrich the couple or the family of the father-in-law. There is also a conflict if the daughter's share of landed property is managed by the husband's family from a different village. There is bound to be litigation and quarrels between sisters and brothers. A better inheritence provision which is rational and equitable would be to evaluate the father's property (movable as well as immovable) or have it declared at the time of daughter's marriage and the daughter's share in rupee value separate from the share of the brothers and other unmarried sisters as well as the parents and any other claimants be announced to the bridegroom as well as the daughter to be married and the amount be regarded as held in trust by the daughter's father/mother/brother who is accepted as trustee by the daughter and her husband. The trust money should then be transferred in well defined instalments to the daughter along with bank rate of interest. This measure will give due rights to women as well as do away with the problems of dowry and also fears about unacceptable fragmentation of the immovable property which ultimately has to be managed by the parental family in the ancestral village. The present legal provisions conferring theoretical equality in inheritence have to be made workable in a society where most of the women become parts of husband's family after marriage. The husband-wife family unit is still restricted only to a small percentage.

Hindu women also now have the right to win a divorce along with the men. Earlier Hindu marriage was not permitted to break apart under practically any circumstances. The Hindu marriage was in general monogamous and now it has been declared legally a monogamous one. The Muslim women could be divorced by a husband very lightly. Recent supreme court decision has made the position of a divorced Muslim woman regarding mainteannce by the ex-husband much better and in line with similar position of other divorced women The Western society it seems has downgraded the institution of marriage and is harvesting a crop of malformed children and a great proportion of broken homes where again the children suffer and the adults seek consultations with the psychiatrists and the yogis. We need not pursue the same course. Better education for happy married life, better interpersonal relations in general and family planning etc., should be included in the curriculm for high school education for boys and girls.

Every now and then there are news of abduction and sale of women. Society must find ways to eliminate atrocities on women. The matter need not rest only with the law enforcement agencies. Perhaps the Arab custom of temporary marriages may help when large number of single men and women have to live singly in cities, Eradication of prostitution often hides certain amount of promiscuity which can only be tolerated if sex education is wide-spread and premarital sex or adultry is not considered completely obnoxious. The cultural compulsion however is for celibacy outside marriage and life-long fidelity to one's spouse. An average Indian male is also very much keen on virginity of the woman whom he may prefer to marry.

It is no longer surprising to see women in all kinds of professions in India. Great majority of marriages in India work out well eventually since the religious theory is for having a marriage for keeps. Much could, in view of this, be said in favour of arranged marriages. The latest version is spoken of as 'self arranged marriages' where after the initial suggestion from almost any quarter and vetting by the parents or elders, the final selection and scrutiny of mutual views is done by the bride or the groom-to-be, themselves. The problem in the industrial society is that the mechanics of arranging introductions is no longer as convenient as it used to be in the past when there was a whole caste of matchmakers serving the householders. The newspapers by matrimonial advertisements are trying to fill the vacuum. In some modernised cities, clubs for youngsters looking for self-arranged marriage partners are being set-up. Some such clubs seem to be meeting the challenge very successfully. Perhaps insurance agents can be assigned the job of keeping track of marriageable young men or women among their client families and make the possible introductions for a fee as a side-line. The insurance company could also have suitable insurance policy for taking care of some of the bride's inheritance from her father if settled at the time of marriage. Certain religious groups and regional festivals have arrangements for collective marriage fixtures in large gatherings.

In India education will be free for girls. Girls eduction should be oriented specially to their problems since the girls have to adjust to a totally strange family after marriage. Education that leads to laziness, pride, cowardice and consumerism may not suit the girls in India. Some special courses in the evolution of family and Indian society should also be taught.

6. Efficiency

If one goes to a private factory for example a famous bicycle manufacturing concern (Hero) of Ludhiana, the workers are engaged on piece rate basis and the production norm is continuously rising. Few years ago the rate was half of what each worker is producing now. The efficiency of workers is quite high in India if the conditions of work, the equipment and the incentives arc right. Sometimes the efficiency per worker is low because very often redundant or booked labour is there but it has no real duties connected with the production. The redundancy and slackness in staff is always necessary to some extent in a country like India where infra-structure of prompt service facilities is limited. But the money efficiency drops mostly where imaginary expenses are shown in books which is now almost universal in the Indian private sector. There is also national need of more jobs and certain link machines are deliberately not provisioned and giant multipurpose machines are fed manually. The use of a partial capacity of machines also makes our industry capital intensive. More than half of the work force engaged in industry or the services is working for the government, and inaction is most convenient in bureau-cracy where laziness can almost never be punished. In the decision making higher echelons of government service, inaction never draws the ire of authority. It is well known Indian mythology that the king of gods is often jealous of human achievement and sets about blocking the final success of mortals. The same philosophy is expressed in the Bible that the exalted ones will be humbled. This is now universal in government service, and many times the bosses are jealous of achievement of their juniors. For winning esteem of seniors kowtowing and a mask of dumb submission are more important : efficiency therefore suffers. There is the spectacle of dozens of functionaries receiving their bosses on routine tours.

The conditions promoting efficiency are primarily the technical and psychological maturity of the managements. The usual conditions are information sharing, participative management, workers welfare as protection from industrial hazards, proper conditions of space, lighting, personal comforts etc. etc. Average production norms should be laid down by work study and there should be competent scheme of incentives.

Best incentives are immediate appreciation and/or financial gain. Merit promotion is not a good incentive, since it can become highly subjective and where it is not considered fair, it might lead to disincentive to others. The promotion to higher rank or pay must be by open competition or by seniority. Merit awards preferably should be one time cash award for any suitable outstanding service. The hardnosed accountants will see that the award is proportional to the event and it should not be something which is at the cost of colleagues like merit promotion or merit increments. Any misfit worker should be retrained for more appropriate job. Continuing education must be used towards better preparedness of the workers.

Besides the incentives and motivation of workers the efficiency will also depend on the efficiency of the tools. Motivation of the workers is essential, since there is the tradition of non-possession and often priority is given to pilgrimages, festivals and semi-religious and social functions like the attendance at marriage etc. If some minimum earning is there, a worker will lightly think of being absent on casual or medical leave or on a protest or strike call by so many authorities to whom he feels owing some allegiance. To overcome such predilictions, there must be more significant propaganda for the culture of work and for national goals. Inculcation of humanism, patriotism, filial attachment and participative group activities strengthen bonds between the managements and the work force. For considerations of efficiency, international competetion must be kept in view. It is on this account that one favours imports especially for the items we make ourselves for the home market and we must export items that may be over expensive for ourselves but which can sell in foreign markets. For meeting this kind of wide competition, we must keep abreast of the advances in technology and give thorough attention to quality and reliability for the prices being charged.

Some of the ills of the industry are on account of social constraints. Competitiveness means self-reliant industry capable of corrective action like merger, expansion, retrenchment, retraining, diversification, bankruptcy etc. Most of our industries are under constraints or special incentives to remain in the inertial status quo. The aim of being viable and giving employment to many or for winning government support for a monopolistic market is the main goal. The overmanning is such that one is pained to observe the production per worker in industry is only double that of the average worker engaged in agriculture or handicrafts. This presumably calls for extensive automation atleast in the capital intensive industries. Non-essential staff must be made to serve elsewhere in some productive service, like adult education or environment upkeep. Trading must be simplified since the consumer has to support a whole chain of traders starting from the factory sale.

7. Justice

Justice delayed is justice denied. If this is true, we have hardly much justice. Justice is independent of executive authority. Our judges are free and conscientious. But the courts where they function are cluttered with work and surrounded by sworn falsehoods. The public is prone to litigation. Many times the higher courts reverse the decisions of the lower courts. This is a challenge to our system of justice that the lower court should do a conscientious job and defer sentence if they also feel that the higher court should look into the matter presumably because of better grasp of law by the lawyers guiding the higher court. Considerably large number of complaints arise because the government officials and public officials are not attentive to matters presented to them by the public. Many times redress of grievances of whole lot of employees occurs through only the intervention of courts. There should be some punishments to officials that initiate mistakes which people will not swallow and the matter goes to court. Most investigations are slipshod and testimony of witnesses false. Under such conditions only persons like Bikram the legendary emperor or Birbal, the wise counsellor of Akbar can give judgements. There is a case for speeding up justice by summary trials by honorary judges appointed for their sagacity and respected position, and a single lawyer who should speak on both side of the case with responsibility for honest legal aid. An extension of Panchayat system for justice could also be experimented with. The dragging of civil disputes in courts for years is highly prejudicial to justice. The government itself has became the biggest litigant and more often than not it supports dishonestly weak cases and often manages to win, throwing a smear on the performance of the system including capability of the judges. The law should also only be a guide allowing freedom to the judge in his evaluation of the case under the broad guidelines of the law.

Legally, caste discrimination, forced labour, bonded slavery, discrimination based on sex etc, have been abolished. In many places however either due to ignorance of their rights, or due to downright nexus between criminals and authorities, or due to vested interests, people still suffer and only certain matters get aired through the press like dowry deaths or the bonded slavery of brickkiln workers. Some of the problems will only be solved if volunteers of progressive national parties take up the matter of securing justice to the weaker sections including the entire public from the guilty bureaucracy. Similarly a citizen consumer movement alone can get redress from the machinations and discourteous dealings of the bureaucracy in the trade and supply area.

Law breaking can be overcome by both strict enforcement as well as converting the laws to be more practical and workable. The repeal of prohibition in most places is an example of dealing with an unpractical law. The generation of black money and non-payment of income tax and custom duties is now being dealt partially by making the laws simpler and by providing incentives as well as disincentives towards compliance and offerring immediate rewards to the custom officials if they successfully book the guilty. Once the prices and financial policies are under good control of the government, individual income tax should become redundant.

Government, being the biggest employer is plagued with disputes regarding working conditions, pay and pension etc of its employees. In general the disputes arise from errors committed by the authorities. The redress of grievances if genuine must automatically be done by the managements, but actually the bureaucratic behaviour prevails and negative action is supported so that no real decision or effort is involved. It is interesting that more often the redress is available only through politicians or courts. This has often been the case even with scientific employees in spite of the government's own science policy resolution favouring the science profession. The scientist managers are also guilty of shirking their responsibilities and blaming there underling administrators. Proper administrative training is also missing in the case of most government administrators who have arisen from the ranks and there is hardly much continuing education. The government is now strengthening the management skills and also is setting up separate departments for dealing with employee complaints and to rid the courts of such work. Punishment of bureaucrats guilty of irresponsible action should be normal when redress is given by courts. (Many times the wrong advice is lightly given by even the law ministry officials to bureaucrats).

Trade unionism a relic of nineteenth century capitalist organization has been plaguing free India in spite of there being a soverign democratic government in the country. The banning of trade unionism from defence undertakings should be extended to all public institutions, making the managements and welfare officers responsible for nipping any grievance in the bud by fair-play. Trade unions in private industries and student associations in universities should be educated to follow the highly motivated and patriotic fervour as in Japan. In the U.S.A. the student association must have its executive body meetings validated by the presence of a non-participating faculty adviser, whose only responsibility is that the association follows its constitution and democratic procedures. In India also any misrepresentation of Indian history or sayings of our great men must be corrected and the guilty persons exposed. Students' economic problems must be dealt with sympathetically by part-time employment and studentships. Students should have a correct perspective of their activities covering professional competence, learning discrimination and debating all kinds of problems facing the country in campus activities and discussion groups.

8

SCIENCE AND NATIONAL GOALS

1. Introduction

It would be worthwhile now to spell out the important national goals and discuss how science and technology may help in achieving these. The indicators of development have been discussed by many authors. For a developing country the indicators will define some of the goals. The indicators are built around economic prosperity, national security, internal peace and the rule of law. Upkeep and husbandry of the environment, good health and longevity, and better status of women indicate also development.

2. External security

The development of the country is thwarted when peace is threatened. India had to divert considerable effort away from development to meet the Chinese incursions in 1962 and to meet repeated Pakistani aggressions. On account of such an experience, considerable resources are continuously being directed towards military preparedness. The major effort of a country which is not a super power, for preserving peace and moulding international climate to suit her interest is by diplomacy and by building friendships. The results of such diplomacy have been the declaration of the five principles of peaceful coexistence and the spread of non-alignment. Indian peaceful stance is a principled one. India has never quibbled with her denunciation of apartheid in South Africa, or of existence of troops on foreign soil whether these be American troops in Granada or USSR troops in Afghanistan or the North Vietnam troops in Cambodia. India has always sided with national integrity whether it is the internal problem in Sri Lanka or the external incursion in Cyprus or the communal strife in Lebanon. One of the chief architects of non-alignment as a policy for all nations big or small was Jawaharlal Nehru who was lauded also for his pragmatic and scientific approach in the long-term interest and self-respect of the nation. At that time it was so easy to sit in the lap of a super power which was actually attempted by some developing countries, but very soon they found this not in the mutual interest of the super power or the small country herself, that attempted to ride piggy-back. A jolt to our policy occurred when the Chinese attempted incursions into Indian territory feeling that since India was equidistant from both the super-powers, perhaps China could win her objectives at the cost of India by force. But soon they discovered that India on the other hand was equally close to both the super powers and China decided to beat a retreat.

India has actually experienced in her brief history as an independent country, unprovoked attacks as many as five times and is having now and then foreign inspired insurgency conditions on her borders. Our thinkers must not feel shy of discussing national policies, potential threats, and alternative strategies for survival, Definite commitment to nationalism and the constitution can alone be tolerated in the border areas. No one may be allowed to hold any other article : a book or a stone or a structure more sacred than the constitution since the constitution gives the freedom and security to practice one's religion and culture in free India. There is no room for the colonial segregation of defence from the national life. Like the developed countries, we must also bring our industry and the institutions of higher learning in the forefront of technological advance in defence science and direction. For example these institutions should carry-out advances in metallurgy, solid state physics, infra-red instrumentation, radar and communication, food packaging and toxicity, personality test batteries, operational research, corrosion and anti-corrosion, oceanography, explosives R&D, aircraft and ship design, composite materials, microelectronics, information theory, advanced mathematics and functioning of satellites, etc. etc. At present on account of the innocence of the universities in many areas, research facilities have been created in special institutions. The suitable universities in the neighbourhood of such institutions should consider establishing certain chairs for defence science.

In order to discourage aggréssion on India, the armed forces have to be kept keyed up to maximum efficiency and armed with best means possible. India has eschewed the use of nuclear weapons. For a peace-loving country, the choice of future enemy is not left to India. The only hope for such countries against the threat of nuclear menace is universal disarmament or the strengthening of the United Nations with military punch. We have the spectacle of the Iran-Iraq conflict where each side accuses the other of escalation. A future antagonist can use any weapons and still claim that they did not use them for offence or they used for saving casualties as the Americans claimed for the Hiroshima bomb. We are openly hostile to Israel and South Africa and we must engage in neutralising their nuclear competence by strengthening peace in the hearts of the world population including the population of these specific countries. There is already a world-wide awareness for the need for outlawing and incapacitating nuclear weapons.

The scientific data published by India on the ill effects and irrelevance of nuclear weapons both for strategic or tactical use is timely and monumental. Nuclear submarines must also be outlawed along with the nuclear weapons, since nuclear depth charges are the natural defence against these and outlawing one should also outlaw the other. Submarine vessels might some day be used for carrying cargo and it should be ensured that even for such peaceful purposes nuclear propulsion is not used.

The inhuman destruction and cruel punishment meted out by radioactive mines and chemical walfare agents is well known and these are regarded as unethical weapons. The outlawing should mean the setting up of a world-wide security agency which could be set up by the non-aligned movement or by any regional-pact countries. The first super-power converted to participation in such world-wide security will naturally earn the gratitude of the entire human race, but such a super power must first disintegrate the skeletons in her own cupboard.

The history of civilization is replcte with slow but sure expansion of civilized states into modern nations from local groupings starting from tribes or petty fifedoms. The regional cooperation being practised in many parts of the world today is a sure sign of maturity in human evolution and soon in mutual interest, viable and almost equally prosperous regional groupings can be expected to usher in an era of international law enforcement. Eventual growth of regional groupings in Europe, Asia, Africa etc. into equally prosperous populations is expected around the mid-twenties of the next century. Such considerations have also prompted the South Asian countries to develop regional cooperation. Such a natural regional scheme is expected to eventually lead to security and peace in the region. The cooperative programme is primarily around the utilization and spread of modern science and technology. Any joint effort will promote break-down of hatred, ignorance and indifference often found among neighbouring countries. Cyclonic storm and flood threat for example to tropical countries can only be met by joint R&D efforts.

Indian support to the establishment of a new economic order and new information exchange system also are steps in the direction of promotion of international cooperation. understanding and peace. Apart from the initiatives in foreign policy, the defence preparedness of any country will depend upon military training and equipment systems based on the technology available to it and developed by it. Wars cannot be won by the preponderance of only one of man-power, equipment or a brave officer corps. Certain mix of all possible means is required, with perhaps an extra capability in certain areas. One of the ways we may out-class a potential enemy is training, and expertise in strategy and tactics which can be ensured by scientific analysis of combat development exercises and their simulation. One is heartened to note the integration of qualified experts in various fields in uniform or outside in these activities. At the time of independence there was hardly any indigenous doctrine or understanding of the why of military tactics. India depended on imported and oudated leaflets from foreign military educational establishments, the supply of which was soon a trickle. Now the tactics are being evolved and proven in our own military establishments. It is not realised outside defence that tactics are based on detailed data of weapon performance and an analysis of many factors affecting this per-performance like, weather, concentration, theory of random numbers, terrain and prior and subsequent action plans etc. Military tacticians develope tactics with the close cooperation of mathematicians and operational analysts, and prove these through games and exercises observed by scientific and technical experts among others.

The science of system analysis and operational research in fact was developed on account of the military needs during the last world war when faced with the then existing faulty tactics of submarine warfare, area bombing, and faulty weapon evaluation or calculation of war wastage rates etc. The Indian planners have done well to recognise the important place of scientific analysis in the system design and performance evaluation as well as evaluation of strategies and tactics. Scientific observers often follow on the heals of advancing battle groups in live wars for future lessons and guidance.

Defence preparedness involves an estimate for future threats and future theatres of war since otherwise the preparedness will only be on the basis of observations relevant to the last war. This future estimation is necessary for basic planning though other contingencies and possibilities have to be kept in the background unlike the French before the world war who planned their defences to hinge on the Maginot line that was bye-passed by the Germans. Futurology panels of scientists and military officers have been established. Futurology however, is not a science but is only built around educated guesses using time projections and theories of statistical analysis of trends and probability of occurrence. Computerised modelling helps in drawing inferences of simulated futures. Often future scenario is very much coloured by the bias of the analyst. A Delphi technique has been invented for questioning and integrating the views of experienced individuals about the future. The foreign provocations (hidden perhaps behind the terroristic happenings) were almost forecast for 1985 more than a few years ago by such techniques. The contingency planning is best carried out by the armed forces headquarters and estimate of mixing such plans at any moment rests with the higher policy making echelons, who have to take the necessary risks and take sometimes bold decisions.

Another important area of application of science in the interest of defence is the organization of scientific investigations of the environment for its detailed structure and quality for use in future operations. Strong groups must actively pursue mapping of the terrian or studies in meteorology, oceanography, glacialogy and study ecosystems like jungles, deserts, river banks, and also subjects like signal propagation, electronic environment and electronic counter measures, survival etc. etc.

Apart from tactics and environment, the weapon systems and the motivation of the user is paramount. The weapon system that we start preparing today can be used only after about 15 years. The German V-bombs were too few to win their war and the American atom bomb almost missed the world war. When the armed forces want to acquire weapon system known to be possessed by a potential enemy, the country then is forced to import similar equipment or its countermeasures and thus be a late comer in such acquisition. It is, therefore, proper to always try to develop advanced and original weapon systems well ahead and thus give oneself an edge say after ten to fifteen years. The period of this development can perhaps be reduced if there is better cooperation and trust between the R&D, users and manufacturers. In peacetime, major part of the gestation period is spent in technical and user trials or production development work. The trials can be assisted by computer simulation and speedier experimental production. The scientists and engineers are also involved in operational training, in storage, transport, maintenance and repair. Considerable technical manpower is tied to the defence effort. This practically non-productive use of any nation's resources will have to continue till some dependable world-wide security system does emerge through acceptance of peaceful coexistence and assigning peace keeping duties to an armed security council. The few countries that obstruct the United Nations in their efforts for consensus towards international treaties for economics, trade, for developmental cooperation or for peace will, we hope, beign to conform by the pressure from their own peace-loving people. A simple test will be the universal adherence to the Law of the Sea treaty recently hammered out by consensus at the suggestion of Malta and initially strongly pushed forward by USA.

3. Internal Security

Peaceful life of a citizen is threatened by ordinary criminal law breakers, and tax evaders, perpetrators of executive and financial irregularities, riots and civil disturbances, terrorists and agitators on all kinds of issues. The techniques of forensic science help combating crime. The first major forensic science laboratory in India was established only in mid-seventies. The police has to have better weapons, mobility and communications. Some of the incapaciating chemical agents to control mobs and rubber ammunition are inventions in aid of the police. India is resorting to engineering structures including border fences, to control illegal immigration. The communist and linguistic disturbances, we hope are practically over and situational synthesis in the Hegelian sense has perhaps taken place. We are still faced however, with communal clashes. This has to be overcome with the spread of secularism and scientific temper.

The scientific temper can be encouraged by well planned public education on scientific enquiry, structure of the cosmos, evolution, history of civilization and humanism etc. This education can be assisted by the Bharat Sadhu Samaj, the itinerant preachers, retired civilian and military personnel by suitable management effort. Weekly discussion groups on announced subjects by suitable people at university campuses and all kinds of clubs can be very useful. The political opportunism has already been curbed by the new act of parliament against defection from the political party on whose ticket one had earlier been elected. The nexus between the politicians and the criminals can only be broken by diligent press and public. The bureaucratic corruption and treacherous espionage is like the darkness under the lamp requiring better security procedures. The proper time to enquire about a government official's income is when any one not necessarily a government official registers purchase of property requiring funds in excess of his salary income of more than three months. The procedure now is to float an enquiry when there is a sale of property or when there is rental etc. income. This allows purchases to be made in some one else's name or in the name of a minor.

Many leaders have stressed the role of character of individuals in the peaceful progress. The education must include character building especially by making the surroundings of a student and the behaviour of teachers and school administration frank and sympathetic. It is also necessary for the educational psychologists and renowned educationists to create the milieu and the course content for such instruction.

The role of press and police in public pillorying of the evil doers responsible for dowry deaths, human scrifice, Harijan baiting and the flesh trade can be crucial. The USSR used to have a ministry of Agitprop for agitations and propaganda in favour of communist practices ; perhaps we should have TV stations entirely devoted to moral education in pallatable form The science of mass psychology, and the very much election generated recipes for attitude moulding ought to be harnessed in this purposeful endeavour.

The public is upset when they hear about the daily toll of traffic and fire accidents, or accidents in factories and accidents during civil construction. Modern technology and attention to proper drills and procedures must be enjoined. Better urban design with collective taxis allowed between centres of sectors and easy renting of bicycles might reduce the density of traffic inside the cities. Private cars should be discouraged except for travel outside the city limits. In Peru certain suburbs require all car owners to park their cars in community garages outside the residential areas and the streets in the residential area are invariably grass lawns. The rail travel can perhaps be made more secure even if it should become more costly and the emphasis on more speed should be less. The trains should be run at economic speeds which are much less than those attempted. Those who are in a rush may be accommodated more by widespread air taxi networks. The delays in waiting at airports can be drastically cut as well as the number of aircraft should be increased for the same service so that there is better maintenance and there is obedience to schedules. The public is exposed to considerable harassment by petty officials and sales outlets of services in private or public sector. The courts could perhaps give licenses as honorary policemen-cum-court-officials against such complaints for summary disposal. Such a device conferring executive duties also on justice officials, cannot be worse than any other possible control and inspection when final say is with the courts regarding obedience to law. Even in minor traffic accidents, under the current dispensation of police investigation, and the repeated procrastination by courts, the net result often is shelling out of money in the court or outside by the well-to-do alleged violator and often the less well-to-do goes scot-free or he might get some money for producing an event for the police or the lawyers, even if objectively the fault lay with himself. The performance of the police must be brought upto a level that the law-abiding public has no inhibitions in approaching them for assistance and for reporting law breaking. Perhaps separate police units should be organised for the duties of security of V.I.P.'s and for ceremonial occasions as we have distinct police bands. The prosecution must be capable and fluent in the use of modern investigative methods and courts must try to eliminate stress on the evidence of witnesses that are usually coached to tell lies on oath. The law could perhaps find a way that the judge can disburse incentives as well as punishments and can reach a just decision than to worry about squaring it with "eye-witnesses" testimony offered by both the prosecution and the defence. Once the judge is settled in his mind, the lawyers concerned should be given appropriate entry in their professional record as to their reliability, to be maintained by the court where they seek to practice.

Safety first has to be a way of life. There are going to be fast modes of travel, universal electrification, increasing automation and the public must be instilled with the safety skills and the fundamentals of the technical and the automated environment. Side-walks must be designed for pedestrians especially women and children unlike the ones at Delhi which invariably have large steps up and down in a short distance and most people use the side of the road than the side walk.

The routine services in the country also are frustrating. There is hardly any bank that will cash a cheque on the dot at 10 A.M., its opening time. One must wait for at least thirty to forty minutes. Post Offices are opened or closed at the whim of the staff. For any meaningful speedy progress, we have to inculcate the work culture in our education and training along with punctuality. Mrs Gandhi almost demonstrated during the emergency that under coercion people do pick up punctuality and simulate culture for work. We are sure, means could be found now also when the emergency is not there to develop these virtues.

4. Employment

Full employment has higher priority when compared to high production. Without proper expansion of employment, higher production will only increase the disparity between the rich and the poor. The prosperity to the extent that some youth are idle and rich, has brought unsocial embitions to many e.g. how the idle but inebriated youth fell prey to the negation of Sikhism by false leaders and foreign agents. It is surprising that even the Sikh scriptures have been interpreted falsely by allotting wrong meaning to some significant words without challenge from Sikh intellectuals. Every 'ardas' begins with an invocation to Bhagwati the Hindu Goddess of power and the principle of energy in God, Bhagwati was also the personal goddess of worship for their founder, but the well known Sanskrit name has been translated tendentiously as 'sword', and this translation completely away from the context of the invocation is taught in the university classes by certain teachers. Apart from re-education in real Sikh faith, the efforts must be made to find more employment for the rural folk in the Punjab who are well informed about the good things of life. The disaffection regarding status quo regarding unemployment in all parts of the country will lead to certain restiveness which may not be contained without considerable effort. The recent Gandhi-Longowal accord which sought an end to violence and terrorism in the Punjab was studded with national commitments to funnel new resources and employment opportunities in the Punjab, though these were already on the cards but there was crisis of confidence between the regional party with limited horizons and the central authority.

Intensive and remunerative agriculture has been made possible by the spread of agricultural scientific and technological knowledge. Large scale agricultural or cooperative inputs and marketing has given it an industrial face. The green revolution is now sought for the whole country. Hybridization of pulses will bring prosperity to dry lands. Better seeds, husbanding of soils, inputs of fertilizers, and pesticides, timely guidance regarding local agricultural operations based on economic and weather forecasts have all contributed to the green revolution. High technology, like the use of radioactive tracers, and labelled compounds have helped in the agricultural and hydrological research. The modernization often has also meant mechanization and use of lifted water by diesel pumps in general and by electric or such means as use renewable resources of energy like the solar energy, bio-gas or wind mills. By the turn of the century India is likely to have about fifty thousand tractors and more than two hundred thousand tube wells. The industrialsation of agriculture will expand.

Small scale self-employment has been the secret of India's wealth in the past and is again being spread far and wide by liberal loans and assistance in appropriate technology. If the educated unemployed, a large proportion of whom are science graduates, can be employed for rural adult education, excellent benefits will follow in the form of better self-employment for newly educated adults. Community radio and TV sets and assistance from village level workers and volunteers from non-official bodies can thus transform the rural scene and provide employment. In fact in order to increase the wages, the production per worker must increase by the use of machines and automation. The consumption of almost anything per capita in India is so low that the internal market can be expanded a great deal. Science and technology are also opening new avenues of wage earning like work for expansion of agriculture and industrial production besides keeping the environment clean, much more exploration and exploitation of the mineral wealth not accessible so far has to be carried out. Jawaharlal Nehru was once heckled in a planning seminar in 1956 by an eminent geologist and was pleased then and there to authorise one hundred scholarships for advanced training in Geology since it was agreed that development must involve exploration of mineral resources in a big way. The work of exploring, extracting and utilising vast marine resources need trained marine geologists, minoralogists and metallurgists besides experts in ocean science and technology. There is indeed dearth of many kinds of specialists and trained technicians. The list below of skill intensive electronic exports to USSR and other socialist bloc countries is very revealing regarding new skill-based jobs that must be arising : the list includes floppy disc drive, semi-conductors, computer periphrals, electronic motors. capacitors, computer software, magnetic recording heads etc., mica plates, telecommunication cables, carbon film resistors, of international quality standards.

Often the jobs are waiting for special skills. Science and technology offers many new work opportunities, e.g., in space exploration, exploration of Antarctica and the oceans, deep see fishing, food preservation and packaging, air-conditioning and cold storage, electronics, computer applications, instrumentation, air-craft industry etc. There is plenty of scope for the expansion of inland air-travel and travel by hovercraft along the coast. Science offers more space to metropolitan coastal cities by linking these by tunnels and bridges to neighbouring islands. Fish farms can be established all along the coast and along rivers. India being the store house of natural plant products can be the natural choice for manufacture of drugs and chemicals. Indian village population provides an almost unlimited market for the products of technology including the high technology. Already steady progress is being made in harnessing solar energy by solar cells for remote villages. The world is poised for break-through in controlled energy from nuclear fusion and catalysed electrolysis of water to give the ideal fuel viz., liquid or compressed hydrogen. The moment these investigations are accomplished, there will indeed be no looking back for the solution to world's problems of energy and employment. More change agents are needed for improving the current handicraft technology. Even the expansion of the bio-gas plants and related lighting and heating appliances can provide work for at least a million people.

When people are trained in science and technology for earning their livelihood, even if they have the peculiar Indian trait of simultaneous acceptance of science as well as dogmas, the humanism and secularism will guide them to avoid postures of hatred or of isolation. Neighbourliness, nationalism and internationalism will all grow.

5. Material resources

The importance of material resources for the progress of civilization can be judged from the fact that various periods of growth have been named after materials like the stone age, the bronze age etc. The current one is the age of tailored materials. High performance materials can be designed by using suitable metal, textile or ceramic fibres and metal or plastic matrix. The chemical industry has produced innumerable plastic materials. The structure variables are the chemical nature of the monomer and the physical nature of the macromolecule like, chain length, side chains, grafts, metal bridges, cross linking pattern and the nature of fillers, and subsequent heat treatment, the stacking pattern, crystallinity, processing parameters, bulk shape etc., etc.

Besides metallic fibres, glass fibres, carbon fibres, polymeric fibres and textiles can be used as reinforcement. Foam plastics are made of many types for packaging, heat insulation and electrical circuit support or for potting. Plastics have replaced cotton and jute for cable insulation. Conventional materials like cotton, jute and paper have been modified to have improved properties for special applications. There is also attention focussed on the use of abundant and renewable material resources, like the agricultural and forest produce and the waste products, sands, muds, clay, stone and marine materials of almost an inexhaustible supply. Materials economy is assured by carrying out miniaturisation and the recycling of materials. Export of minerals and rare metals should be controlled and reduced. Considerable R&D is still necessary in the use and application of amorphous semi-conductors and super-conductors. Magnetic materials of great variety are available. Recently a 'carbene rubber' has been invented in India which will not catch fire and can be a boon for military applications. Simple living, the ideal of Indian thinkkers is now the in-thing for conservation of materials.

Modern industry has many applications of glass, glass like plastics and ceramics. India imports a great many sophisticated materials, magnets, crystals, silicon chips, copper coated iron wire, rare metal ribbons, special steels and alloys etc. There is so much scope for production on small scale by R&D laboratories and it is the production of such materials which really provide advanced technology and instrumentation, otherwise we are going to remain technologically dependant. At present priority is for bulk production of common materials.

We have elsewhere dealt with coal and oil in connection with energy. Large quantity of copper, aluminium, steel etc. are required for generation of electricity and its transmission. Because of scarcity of copper many aluminium alloys with suitable additions and treatments have replaced copper in certain applications. Electronics industry is the cottage industry of the future. The development of essential crystalline or amorphous semiconductors and the technology of large scale integration must become common-place in the country. We are only using imported microprocessors. Much hope is centered around the efforts of Bharat Electronoics and the Semiconductors Ltd.

An important area of materials techology is production of

single crystals and production of optical glass. We have developed optical glass and can make single crystals of various kinds in laboratories. The special materials and instruments is a field where research groups and schools all over the country should join for making batches and proto-types.

6. Food and Housing

Alleviation of wide-spread hunger and availability of appropriate housing depends primarily on the removal of poverty, and holding the price of essential requirements within reach of vast majority of the people. A large number is below the poverty line and therefore cannot efford even the necessities of life. The provision of remunerative employment has already been dealt with. The state organisation at village level must invole itself entirely in development activity including the distribution of credit and appropriate technology, organization of cooperatives, distribution of raw materials and marketing of produce. Every rural institution should be a window on some rural activity and not just be a bundle of registers. There should be tremendous market for ready-made foods among the city folk. Midday meals for children besides providing the required nutrition would also be a tool for moulding the habits and tastes for clean and wholesome food in the population. The expected large catches of marine food will require about ten-fold expansion of the market for fish. India is an exporter of many food items and the expansion of food production is keeping pace with the increase in population which is likely to stabilise in the next fifty years or so. The exports are however, at the cost of own population since the buying power at present is rather low.

The urbanisation is very ancient but now every village has the aspiration to be a city and science and technology can make it possible. Science and technology offers better town planning and civic services, better communications, electricity, telephones, computer terminals and better security services. When we come across the spectacle of recently constructed fine houses in dirty town streets across the length and breadth of the country, we become conscious of the shortcomings in our method of working and indifference to better social action and better engineering practice.

Future cities will be decentralised and never allowed to go

beyond a certain size. This is possible with new means of communications, visual phones and televised meetings. Specialised services and business can be concentrated in certain towns. Industry must spread out over the entire country. Growth of slums is only a relic of by-gone backward ages and will slowly vanish. New construction materials and designs of housing to suit every one are now being developed. There is need of dissemination of knowledge through district organizations rather than only from Delhi or from a few learned institutions. Life of timber can be increased by many treatments including exposure to nuclear radiation. Use of composite materials based on cheap fibres and mud can save costs. Mass produced plastic sheets can serve as roof covers. Vehicular traffic can be diverted from populated areas as has been attempted at Chandigarh.

7. Climate and Environment

Climate of most of the country is mild. Only a portion is desert or is snow bound. Citizen rights have been sought to be curtailed by regionalism e.g. in Hyderabad and in Bombay at one time but regionalism is in retreat. There is however, constitutional regionalism in only Jammu and Kashmir and protective regionalism in Arunachal Pradesh, in Nicobar islands and in other tribal forests. The democratic nationalism must be alert to thwart attempts of regionalism to grow as in the Punjab, Assam, Manipur etc. Regional prejudices will hinder the growth of a single Indian nation made of diverse cultures.

Science and technology assures modification of both micro- as well as macro-climates. Electric fans, humidifiers and air-conditioning can give desired climate in the dwelling at the flick of a switch. If the unemployed youth of the country engage themselves in constructing and supplying etc. of climate modifiers to all householders, they will be engaged on this work almost for ever. Cold storage has influenced the marketing and production of vegetables, foods, fruit, milk, meat, fish etc. tremendously. The expanded market both in time as well as in area for a single gathering of fresh produce has brought prosperity to producers and transporters and also necessary nourishment to people. The former local seasonal glut and scarcity elsewhere is now a thing of the past. The market is only being scratched and many people are not getting nourishing fresh food, primarily because of wide-spread poverty requiring simultaneous action on many fronts to supply work as well as food at one's door.

Rainfall is an important ingredient of climate as well as it has great significance for the life style of the people. India has the wettest and practically the driest place in the world. Barring the heavy rains in the north-eastern region and the western coastal strip south of Bombay, the rest of the country has medium rainfall (with the exception of the Indian desert in Rajasthan). Since the rain-fall is seasonal and the farmers depend on the correct timing of sowing their crops with respect to its onset, the meteorological forecasts especially of rainfall are very important. The meteorologists can attempt fairly successfully the fore-casts about rainfall as well as winds, temperature etc. Experiments to induce rainfall have been successful under certain favourable conditions which do occur in Gujarat, Madhya Pradesh and Orissa. When the clouds are of the right type and above the area of interest, the clouds can be seeded by scattering some salt nuclei in it by means of aircraft, or rockets. Silver iodide salt performs best. Hydrology investigates and charts underground water resources. Geophysical methods are employed to determine underground proximity of water. In a non-technical way, water diviners relying on some peculiar sensitivity of their own limbs could point out buried wells or reservoirs Such gifted people are still around.

For withstanding the inclement cold in the Himalayan Regions, special layered clothing with insulation or radiation reflecting layers has been designed. Electric blankets can be useful at night if electric mains are available. Light plastic blankets with retention of body warmth have been designed for outdoor work. For high altitude flying where cold vacuum exists, special flying suits and pressurised canopies are used. Technology is available for deep diving bells and pressure withstanding hulls for the ocean. Cave dwellings and houses on stilts are used in special habitats.

Whereas the climate is the environment provided by nature. Pollution of the environment is man-made. Any harmful gases and natural pollution near marshes or volcanoes are naturally avoided, but the human engineered pollution is insidious and occurs more where people have to live and work. When the population of the world was small, the abuse of the environment could be tolerated to some extent, only now when the pollution exceeded bearable limits, the people awoke to the danger of man eliminating himself by making the environment intolerable. The rivers of Europe and America became almost sewage drains and inland seas near the coasts became health traps as well as killers of fish and marine life. The sea food became contaminated and caused disease in coastal communities as happened in Japan. The old indifference gave way to concern since the scale of pollution has multiplied with wide-spread urbanization and industrialisation. Recently India has set up a Ganga purfication project with American assistance. Large cities like Calcutta, Bombay and Delhi, have realised the growing industrial pollution. The Taj needs protection because of the chemical pollution in the atmosphere on account of oil refinery close by. The spot pollution from industrial stacks and effluents can be controlled by social expenditure by the industries concerned. There are well known successes. The Century Rayon has managed to rectify the obnoxious smells around it in Kalyan. The fish have returned to the Thames on account of stringent anti-pollution measures adopted by the British industry. In India a great problem exists because of the unhygienic conditions all over the country and particularly acute conditions in large cities with their symbiotic slums. The present day technology can however assure that resources spent on biogas, sewage works and waste management can assure hygienic and clean surroundings as well as energy, fertilizers etc. useful bye-products. There are also great possibilities of employment of properly trained people. It is incumbent on the people of India to preserve the habitat for the coming generations. Preservation and improvement of soil and forests have to be particularly looked after.

Mahatma Gandhi wisely stressed the importance of waste management problems in the villages. The bio-gas production has given a most desirable incentive as well as a tool. The latrine-cum-bio-gas-structures have to be designed and placed almost at every few kms of the rural landscape. The people have to be educated to prefer these latrines than the use of open spaces in the present day crowded country-side where there can be no privacy, and incidentally the neighbourhood gets proper fuel and fertilizer. The use of cow-dung and other wastes can also augment the production of bio-gas in private plants based on large cattle sheds. The new devices could never be developed when the country groaned under the yoke of untouchability and the scavenging could be forced on the unfortunate untouchables. Now the technology has come to the aid of the people by making scavenging clean and socially beneficial to all. Appropriate technology is spreading in the craft of scavenging and waste disposal. Even the current continuing pollution of our rivers has to be reversed and eliminated altogether. Already the anti-pollution drive for the holy Ganges has begun with assistance of the international community.

The National Institute of Occupational Health (Ahmedabad) and its two regional centres at Bangalore and Calcutta are engaged in studies on the environmental and occupational health hazards. The hazards arise in many industries e.g., from dust in slate pencil industry, quartz crushing units, mineral extraction and coal based industries, glass industry etc. or chemical toxicity in chemical and dye industry, metallurgical industry etc. Simple precautions like using gloves could ameliorate the nicotine exposure of workers in tabacco fields and industry. The country is using large quantities of chemical fertilizers and pesticides and public has to be aware of the toxicity hazards from residues. Public health staff is also being trained to handle cases of depression, an affliction which is in an epidemic form in the affluent countries on account of increased isolation of individuals facing changing environment of artificial light and sound and lonely pastimes. Malaria is still not under control excepting in certain pockets, but there is some hope of success through biological control under investigation by the Indian Council of Medical Research.

8. Information and scientific temper

Modern living demands speed in acquisition and conveyance of information. The spread of telephones and telegraph all over the country can be foreseen to bring about a transformation in our life as well as to provide millions of new jobs. More expansion should be possible if private enterprise is allowed in this industry so far reserved for the public sector. The government run telephones have not been a roaring success and some differently managed service might be useful for some competition in the interest of consumers. The new services have to be run on commercial basis. New technologies based on tropospherical scatter, optical fibres carrying modulated light beams, laser repeater stations, satellite bounced waves, all can have a place in the shapes of things to come in our vast country. The better channels of communication can make education of the people also a reality. Universities will also impart professional instruction in appropriate technology and education for all will also prepare them as citizens of a secular, democratic and socialist country. Character, simplicity and humanism have to be rebroadcast from our seats of learning for the young minds.

Newspapers are regarded as an essential service in a free democracy. In developed countries every village has a newspaper. The demand for news-papers will increase with increase in the literate population and the village newspapers must strengthen the literary capability of newly educated adults. Newsprint and small printing presses are now manufactured in the country and supply is sure to keep pace with the demand. So much forest waste like leaves etc. can be used for hand made paper and some news sheets could perhaps use such materials. Cheap micro-printed copies of well known news papers could be sent to every primary school and easily projected there for students to read. India and most developing countries have supported UNESCO efforts for unbiased dissemination of news which has not the blessings of some developed countries who are so used to their monopoly of news and views vending. Scientific attitude cannot support biased dissemination of news and propaganda in the interest of the few entrenched classes in different lands. Greater internal communications and exchange of views is necessary for the proper reflection of popular wishes in the individual decisions of the state.

Computerised information systems are increasingly used in industry, offices and in libraries etc. The increase in the use of computers increases human capacity and strength through greater information at their beck and call. Many institutional and commercial worldwide data banks can be tapped by authorised agencies through the use of computer terminals. Enormous effort will have to be made to provide computer services for almost any and everyone for their professional and social needs.

S cientific temper is expected to be nourished with the

increased awarness of science. Science is the major agent for cultural enlightenment. Sir Watson Watt has called it the greatest of the humanities. According to Fritz and Vicky, the most important social contribution of science has been to dispel the aberration of the human mind and for substitution of trustworthy knowledge for superstition and dogmas.

The social conditions determine value system and for convenience and survival the values dear to the individual would conform to the value system. Slowly due to change in society and influence of outstanding individuals who could be in tune with the evolving future, the values change. The value system is based on cultural mores, traditions and influence of charismatic leaders. The changes in political and cultural environment and advances in science and technology will not bowl-out the individual who takes kindly to such changes. Importance of rituals gave way to materialism and humanism. Loyalty to feudal superior has given way to equality and respect for knowledge, skill or piety. Due to such changes certain groups change self-image of relative importance and also assume different relative positions. In modern times heirarchy is replaced with equality and virtue has begun to reside in riches. The human worth is often measured by one's possessions. The change in values, thrusts different people to positions of leadership in the society. The heirarchical system enjoined people to increase their vassals. This was the common background of the Indian polity upto modern times. Napoleon is the classical example of the heirarchical system. Mahatma Gandhi and Jawahar Lal Nehru and others of the re-awakening were the architects of the new value system that resulted in freedom of India. It is upto the present Indians to accept only such changes as may assure further development and prosperity of India. It is here that greater accent must be placed on scientific temper.

Science and technology have changed the face of the country. The people have ready access to knowledge and power. Electrification is the real revolution that has abolished universal drudgery and underpins the abolition of slavery and removal of untouchability or the struggle against apartheid. Pluralism is no longer a threat to society since the society itself is on the democratic path of equality and consensus. New psychological discoveries confirm the human mind as capable of simultaneously favouring divergent philosophies. Such a state can have an apt parallel with the states in Physics.

Scientific temper enjoins peace, coexistence, search for better explanations and accepting diversity of mental levels of different individuals as well as existence of such different levels in the same individual. Scientific temper can understand the progress of evolution in civilization, in history and even in a single individual. Scientific temper is strengthened by the knowledge of the astrophysical concepts, understanding of interaction of particles, transformation of energy and mass. Scientific temper acceps tentatively, existing theories and seeks better theories for explaining and forecasting new facts. Search for absolute theories is part of scientific outlook. Prof Weinberg has offered the values in science as a possible model for values in human affairs. The underlying value in science is truth which is also the basic human value according to most philosophers. Is it not a challenge for society to base itself on truth and to overcome falsehood ? Same applies to scientific search for unity and that can also be a basic human value.

9. Recreation and health

With increasing health and longevity, the people will have more leisure. Recreation has to be planned better so that it is conducive to health and well-being. Recreation must be for all age groups or mixture of certain age groups. The television is an excellent educational and recreational aid for the entire family. It has already become very popular. The colour television and three dimensional televisions will also spread. In India cinema is still the entertainment for great majority. Many families do not have private sets and it is not so easy to pick and choose television programmes in India since in general there is a single channel. There appears to be greater chance for the 3D cinema and the Czechoslovakian style of cinema-theatre mix, in which the actors appear on stage and at certain episodes in the drama the same actors continue the action on screen. Live theatre has always been very much alive in the form of religious plays and single actor deliveries. As often suggested by the late Prime Minister Mrs. Indira Gandhi, group singing can become a participative and nation-building entertainment par excellence.

West Europeans are in the fore-front of participative sport

distinct from competive sports. The folk games of hide and seek, or hunter around the circle are popular participative games in the country. The developed countries are pushing the computer games both as an education as well as an entertainment. Betting and gambling in the form of the lotteries are now quite entrenched. Yogic exercises have now proven their merit even for the training and fitness of space crews. Science confirms the claims of the yogis. Yoga and yogic practices should be upwrapped from mystic veil so that one and all can benefit without too much dose of philosophy or ritualistic preparations. Yoga is essential for healthy old age without the threat of artesclerosis.

India has given to civilization the habits of daily bath, care of the teeth, morning walks, and the pleasures of morning and evening meditation. The Indian poets from Kalidesa to moderns have indulged in most beautiful poetry in appreciation of beauty as well as deep fancies of mind. It has been fashionable among Hindi and Urdu knowing gentry to write philosophical and love poetry. Most Indian temples are located among scenes of great natural beauty and they provide the backdrop for pilgrimages and considerable tourism. Inter-regional and international goodwill is generated by contented tourists. Recently international tourism has been advised to combine visits to temples and monuments with modern sports and recreation like mountain climbing, trekking in the wild, bird watching and photographing Odysseys, visits to wild-life preserves, marine national parks as well as fairs and festivals. The tourists soon learn that poverty does not inhibit poor Indians from being hospitable and that inside even mud hovels and in personal life style the people love cleanliness, but most people are quite careless about civic hygience and the tourists also may have to bear with this lack of social virtue.

India is self-sufficient in her requirements of food and nutrition. With medical advances we are assured that our norms are now adjusted to the culture and life-style of the people, though our per capita consumption of milk and animal protein is almost the least in the world. However, with the new scientific advancement in agriculture in the country, the increase in production of milk, cattle and grains has been very impressive and already we are exporting many varieties of food. Internal consumption will definitely rise with increasing prosperity. All medical care systems are flourishing and now the state also gives support to various scientific and empirical systems. There is quite an integrated approach as far as the patients are concerned who will try any system one after the other or sometimes two of them simultaneously. The practitioners of modern medicine which draws major state support, are now taught also elements of Yoga and are debarred from using well known Ayurvedic, homeopathic or Unani medicines and preparations. The other systems have in their curricula, regular courses in modern sciences and modern medicine. For chronic cases, homeopathy has become quite popular and its practice is fairly common-place by rich people who treat people without charge and also give free medicines which are even otherwise extremely cheap and suit the poor population. All the systems trust the modern methods of diagnosis. The instruments are usually best used by allopathic doctors and the diagnosis is then the starting point of the treatment by any kind of doctor.

The medical instrument industry in the country is only in its infancy. A tremendous expansion of modern medical facilities is required. The rural population will require special hospitals on wheels and travelling medical workers.

Poverty is the major problem endangering health in India. Still agency efforts and voluntary work is reaching information about prevention of disease, hygiene, family planning etc to a large proportion of the population. Epidemics have been controlled and small pox eliminated. Malaria, leprosy, tuberclosis and many endemic diseases in the past have found suitable treatments. New drugs purely based on Indian efforts are few inspite of considerable R&D funds being spent, primarily because of the promotional superiority of multinationals. Some national effort in the production of Indian formulations is called for with cheaper access to advertisement media. The public has to be educated into preferring guaranteed medicines of suitable national and cheaper makes. Though medical care is the cheapest in the world here, yet it is beyond the pockets of most to find adequate hospital beds and quality medicines at proper prices. The government is promoting family planning whole heartedly and contraceptives and family planning advice is readily available. Luncheon schemes for school children, their periodical medical checks and other social services are freely available in the cities and in some rural centres.

The social evil of drug adultration is often ecountered but the laws now are quite tough when some one is caught. The foreign companies have profited a great deal by selling their patented formulations by the dint of hard work in sales promotion. India pharmacoepia committee is well advised to draw up specifications for the drugs on the basis of performance or chemical names rather than physical formulations.

Mahatma Gandhi was a strong supporter of naturopathy and preventive health discipline against disease. Health education and preventive measures should be part of general education and part of training of health workers.

Mental health problems increase with the complexity of civilization and required skills and abilities tend to overwhelm some people. There is increasing problems faced by newly married women partly because the ability to earn a living has been added to many other expectations including house-hold drudgery. Indian environment with absence of guilt about original sin, belief in reaping the fruit of deeds in this or the past lives, respect for mendicants, merit in listening to religious texts and discourses and respect of elders contribute to fewer mental disorders. On the other hand, poverty, harassment in general, close identification with others, public disturbances and agitations cause new unbalances. The cults and gurus within civilized bounds are good for mental health of marginal cases. This is also the experience of the developed countries. So-called fiudamentalist interpretation (rather mis-interpretation) of religion is also a sign of mental ill-health like that of the times that saw in Germany the growth of Hitlerite Nazism, To fight communalism which is also of the same kind, mass communication experts, opinion moulders and psychologists have to assist the society.

The Indian Council of Medical Research is engaged fairly successfully in developing counter-measures against common diseases and epidemics encountered in the country. There are about a hundred medical R&D establishments and research groups engaged in this work. There is however some lacuna in basic medical research because the funding of medical academic work in colleges is poor and such institutions are in the same rut as many an old engineering college, the emphasis being only on imported and out of date text-book ridden degrees.

10. Space Science

The beginning of space science effort was in the experiments on rockets and missiles during the world war. After the war, the allies went all out in excelling each other in rocketry and ballistic missiles. Russia surprised the whole world by sending aloft heavy loads in the from of sputniks. America followed by projecting many satellites and soon a man was landed by them on the moon. Russian sputniks, American international communication and weather satellites, The American space shuttle and, photography from close encounters of distant planets have been landmarks in space develpments. Multi-warheaded missiles with individual target planning, Mr. Reagen's star war programme for anti missile defence are the dangerous aspects of space science. India is against the militarisation of space and places value on the peaceful uses of space science and space satellites.

It was the farsight of Dr. Vikram Sarabhai and his colleagues that with the political support from Mrs Indira Gandhi, space research facilities were planned in the country. A space research station at Thumba was set up initially for ground observations of satellites and later rocket research was begun under international auspices for disseminating space science to developing countries. The Indian space science facilities include Vikram Sarabhai space centre at Trivandrum, SHAR rocket range facility near Madras, a Satellite centre at Bangalore and Space Applications centre at Ahmedabad. India already has Indian made satellites rocketed in space with the help of suitable American or Russian rockets fired from their soil. Within a couple of years India will be rocketing into space its own satellites.

Major Indian Space Mission projected for 1985-1995

(From the Annual Report of the Department of Space)

Mission	Projected for the Year (one Each)				
SROSS & ASLV	1985	1986	1987	1989	
(Stretched Rohini Satellite and Augmented Satellite Launch Vehicle)					
IRS & Procured Launch		1986	1988		
IRS & PSLV at SHAR		1988	1990	1992	1994
(Indian Remote Sensing Satellite, Polar Satellite Launch Vehicle)					

INSAT & Procured Launch	1986	1988	1990		
GSLV Test Launch			1991		
INSAT & GSLV				1992 1993	1995

(Indian National Satellite and Geostationary Satellite Launch Vehicle)

Already television has spread to nooks and corners of the country with the use of stationary satellites. India is in a position to use satellite navigation and position fixing according to their limited needs. Remote sensing is an important use of space satellites. The Indian Remote Sensing Agency at Hyderabad with a division at Dehradun is using photo-transmissions from international satellites for data collection and planning purposes. Instrumented observations from satellites can give synoptic parameters for the oceans and the atmosphere and such interpretation is now being done at Hyderabad, Delhi and Goa of transmissions from INSAT and other satellites. Remote sensing from space can assist agriculture, pest control, weather and marine climate forecasts, mineral exploration, fisheries research, control of disease and disaster alleviation and warning.

11. Emerging Technologies

We must come abreast with the world in technology, but we need not pursue the same tortuous path which has been traversed for example by a developed country like the United Kingdom in the past 300 years at their historical speed. We have naturally to condense the time span. An important direction of progress would be to jump to a concentrated effort in some chosen emerging technologies. So that we can give and take as equals in such work with colleagues in developed countries. Some of the emerging technologies are : biological control of pests, optical fibres, remote sensing, bio-technology, automation and robotics, sea-bottom mining, controlled nuclear fusion, food and fish preservtion by radiation, etc., etc. Mastery of any new technology gives new confidence and new jobs. Recently a National Bio-technology Board has been established to promote projects involving genetic engineering, bio-catalytic systems, cell hybridization and enzyme engineering etc. often having a bearing on agriculture, medicine and chemical manufacture through fermentation etc.

Prof. V.L. Ginzberg had completed a list of key problems

of Physics in 1974 as follows :

(a) Macrophysics : Controlled nuclear fusion, super conductivity at higher temperatures, metallic hydrogen, liquid semi-conductors, high power lasers etc.

(b) Microphysics : Mass spectra of particles, space quantization, particle interactions at ultra-high energies, violation in C P invariance, non linear phenomena in vacuo in ultra strong electro-magnetic fields.

After ten years these problems are still important. The project proposals in such important areas could receive higher priority in basic research. It is such work in new fields and technologies that will measure our maturity as a technological force in the world. Market considerations need not determine the forcing of pace in new technologies. In the past also international developments of aeronautics, space science, or jet aircraft, have come about by governmental efforts. New science policy and industrial policy determine such thrusts which have considrable social returns and not just a profit on investment. With a view to fully take into account social costs, merit of the future product will enjoin work in new technologies.

There is the danger of intertia creeping in the pursuit of new technologies, since any admission of technological error is not considered politically safe when a scientific decision may require curtailment of the project. Thus a high level scientific monitoring of progress and the goals has to be in existence.

Along with the progress of work in new technologies, there should be parallel effort in technology utilization in a programme for channelling the fall-out into industry. Atomic Energy Department has carried out best programme of this kind. Other agencies like the CSIR or DR&DO and space R&D may also energise such programmes as they also have many laboratory results useful for industry if suitable development effort can be added. The Atomic Energy Department's secret of success was unilateral decision to provide development funds.

Technological innovations and progress are essential for the take-off and the forging ahead of the economy. Studies on the organizational impact, environment impact, employment situation and quality of life, will be necessary for political endorsement.

9

PROMOTION OF SCIENCE AND TECHNOLOGY

1. Introduction

Science and Technology in India is a growing colossus. The progress depends on the basic processes of creativity, innovation and decision making. In this chapter we shall deal with the factors influencing these processes. Formulation and progressing of plans will depend on the choice of the projects and on system approach, PERT, net-work analysis, suitable controls and evaluation or in other words choice of correct strategy and tactics. We shall also deal with the mechanics of transfer of technology from the laboratory in India or from the supplier of technology outside the country to the manufacturer. Science and technology will help our people to live a simple and comfortable life in the near future in a climate of freedom.

For any deliberate progress, qualitative and quantitative projection of needs and resources is necessary. A strong information system is required. Lord Mayo (Viceroy of India 1861-1873) set up the Department of Knowledge and Statistics and successor departments have now expanded considerably. We also need forecasts of new inventions and changes in environment. The best way is to sound views of experienced and knowledgeable people in various fields. The Delphi technique coloured somewhat by the views of the investigator, identifies possible developments and from views of experts, the probabilities of occurrence are assigned. Cross impact analysis determines the internal consistency of these probabilities. The forecasts can then be included as per the national policy in the planning. The Baye's theorem is used to update such probabilities in view of new information received later. The best way is to have a rational mix of objectives. For deterministic or large systems, the forecasts can be made well ahead, but for the stochasic systems often encountered in planning, the non-stationarity allows us prediction with only a short lead time. Forecasting is often assisted by the attention given to related processes e.g., the forecasting of earthquakes by observations of magnetic declination. Analogies can also help the mathematical analysis e.g., prediction methods of intensification of agricultural pests will also apply to the appearance of crisis situations in the world, endangering peace. Automatic correction ln plans might be attempted by feedback, but corrective action will be slow, as there is belated response in large systems. It would be better to perform numerical experiments. Renewal theorem of statistics investigating probability of repetition of historical phenomena should apply but for the changes identified or not identified in advance. Progress in management technology like the increases in communication valency or the channel capacity can influence the progress of the plans.

2. Creativity, innovation and decision making

Creativity is the seed of progress and the start of the innovation chain. Decision points are located all along the chain linking various activities. Innumerable studies have been made regarding the factors that might influence creativity. The mental processes that lead to creativity are highly characteristic of the individual and general mental exercises cannot be identified that enhance an individual's creativity. Supra-consciousness of the state of 'Samadhi' is also recognised as being creative, but the success in this endeavour depends in part on chance or God's grace. No quantum of time or effort is fixed before hand for success. Still acceptance of the preparatory life-style, undivided attention to the task and intense desire to succeed are helpful. The creativity in scienc might result from a careful study of possible questions and conceptual connections that require elucidation. One must be abreast of the frontier of knowledge in the field of interest along with wide awareness of advances in other fields. The first creative glimpse is intuitive and is partly due to the working of the subconscious mind. A creative individual is devoted to exploring any new approach including his own intuitive one and does not block progress by self-inhibition and imagined or real difficulties. He is not totally discouraged by the obvious conflict with generally accepted ideas or the frown from his colleagues and superiors. The judgement on new ideas is deferred until he is prepared to completely accept or reject them in view of the evidence or projections. Often the experimental or theoretical support is collected afterwards. Some creative ideas are so convincing that the idealogue succeeds in pushing them to tentative acceptance by others even when no proof in the usual sense may exist. Most revelations are examples of this nature of creativity.

Certain psychologists observing the hard and penurious lives of certain creative people often beset with initial non-acceptance and rejection have advanced the concept that hardship and compulsion would perhaps nourish creativity. There is the example of certain industrial R&D groups producing creative ideas and new products when threatened with termination of jobs on account of impending bankruptcy or merger of the industry in question. The proper explanation is that adversity acts as a filter in favour of near successful ideas and also expedites announcements, when otherwise one might be proceeding leisurely in the hope of getting more important results. From large number of observations on creative scientists, it is now held that creativity is entirely unpredictable, intuitive product of highly trained and motivated individuals. Pursuit of creative ideas to some useful outcome depends an the environment which, if it is adverse, can bury creativity. An example often is given of the poor creative environment in Indian research, since same scientists are much more creative when visiting or working abroad than when at their own desks in India. Perhaps one is positively influenced by the creative output of the colleagues and one needs interaction with others well-versed in the advanced field or related fields. For India where many creative scientists work in isolation, travel funds for lectures and discussions about unpublished or published work must be placed at the discretion of Directors of research laboratories for assisting gifted individuals to travel and speak at other research centres. This along with other visits of well known experts will have a catalytic effect.

Creativity is aided by the appreciation and attention from colleagues and superiors. This is now available in most laboratories in India. But in the beginning, quite a few scientists did experience jealousy and suppression by their senior colleagues. This jealousy and suppression has to be deliberately extinguished by the efforts of suitably trained R&D directors and project leaders. Indian mythology is also replete with stories how the chief of gods out of jealousy thwarted the success of great mortals. We have to steer our managers away from such interference. The psychologists have discovered that restriction to a limited field is not conducive to creativity. One must pursue other studies and activities also. A gifted person does not experience interference from other secondary activities but receives synergism. Proven creative people are considered extremely valuable in developed countries and are provided facilities for thinking and experimenting so long as they wish. In India general appreciation is yet lacking and mediocrity flourishes widely. The general atmosphers of graft and subjective thinking has often spoiled even the objectivity expected from scientists. Though the skeleton of peer-review, refereeing and motions of arriving at decisions in a committee are followed, but true recognition of merit is only accidental. Creative people are somewhat aloof and self-sufficient and often held as odd balls mainly because they have no patience for usual pastimes of flattery and back-bitting. Well known creative Indian scientists have been Saha, Raman and Bose. They hardly could play any part in the phenomenal expansion of science and technology in the country, though they were always extremely popular with their students and colleagues in the research laboratories. We also have the example of Prof. Oppenheimer of USA and many scientists in Stalin's Russia or Hitler's Germany who could not flourish in the normal manner.

There is no specific aptitude for creativity and therefore it is not easy to spot creative individuals or potential creativity. From hindsight one could hazard the guess that correlational efficiency somewhat indicated by the inkblot tests and verbal fluency score high for the creative people. The screen picture of a creative scientists or artist being a dissipate is incorrect. A creative director of a research laboratory is extremely valuable for the country and is not easily replacable. The creative output is large around a creative leader of science. Our universities often lack participative management of research which stays fragmented. A group in the laboratory means an interacting and mutually instructive group. Many of the universities lack such groups. The scientists usually are content to plough their lonely furrows, it is only the leadership which creates interactive groups and future leaders.

Creativity demands flexibility and critical faculty along with insight and hard work. The ancient poets and prophets were intensely creative, but the same cannot be said of the faithful diehards or fundamentalists who forget the revolutionary origin of their dogma and would stifle all criticism or fresh thinking. Science accepts any belief only as the starting point for progress that may eventually even topple today's beliefs. Normally human beings transacend the plurality of beliefs and permit coexistence of conflicting ideas in their individual or communal minds. It is on account of scientists being non-fundamentalist in the accepted sense of the term, that they can also be anchored in faith or ethical values. Einstein has been a shining example of this.

For Keynesian prosperity around sufficient production and sufficient employment, the progress of science and technology and therefore of underlying creativity is crucial. However a specific creativity or basic advance will lead to prosperity through employment and production only through the successful functioning of the innovation chain in the society in question The innovator is the person (often distinct from the creative scientist or technologist) who identifies the product or the need likely to be met by the creative ideas. The industrial revolution in England was mainly brought about by artisan inventors and innovators. The innovator then arranges for the techno-economic survey for the product or service in view, and manages production development in association with engineering consultants and if possible some financier and industrialist or entrepreneur. The market development and sales are also links in the chain. The learned journals and the appropriate departments often discuss that the British and Americans have come up with creative ideas in science and technology but industrial exploitation or the innovative inputs have been superior in West Germany or in Japan. Perhaps the cultural environment and self-estimate inspite of the defeat in the last war was conducive to this. They also point out that the effort on the remaining chain after the identification of the useful science and technology is about ten times that went into the formulation of the basic scientific or technological contribution.

The successful production is beset with decision making at various points. Which process should be used depending on the available raw materials, equipment, finances, time frame, skills etc. ? The scale of manufacture has to be determined and initially experimental production pursued. Our large scale steel plants if used at a fraction of their useful capacity on account of miscellaneous reasons like low technical proficiency, dearth of standard raw materials, shortage of power or contraction of demand or increase in the cost of transportation to customers, would mean a loss on account of heavy investments made initially. At every decision point, comparative model analysis, decision tree calculations, and systems approach are necessary. Many processes may have hidden social costs or adverse environmental impact that eventually might smother the project.

The national decisions for major projects have to be taken after full consideration of the possible social or environmental impact. The advice of scientists can be fairly definite under the defined state of nature and defined constraints. The technical advice is different from the legal advice where different lawyers can support diametrically opposite verdicts or where different courts one higher than the other can arrive at diametrically opposite verdicts. The considered technical advice is probabilistic depending on the constraints etc., and the decision maker has to use the same as a guide only. Since the responsibility is of the decision maker, he might rely on his own feelings about the matter and be prepared for the consequences. Most decisions are unique and therefore alternatives cannot be realistically compared as only one alternative can occur in the physical world.

Creative management and creative marketing that involve new concepts or new combinations of existing constructs have a great role in the success of the innovation chain. Many countries including India are now becoming alive to the importance of earmarking resources for the innovative process. In a developing country attention has to be given to the use of local scientific and engineering talents along with the know-how available from abroad. This is the problem of purchase and transfer of technology to the production managers. In-house R&D or the one available nearby will get assimilated much better. It was only after long apprenticeship that the Engineer India Ltd. could come abreast of modern technology in petrochemicals from abroad. The United Nations have stepped-in to suggest a draft model agreement for technology transfer from transnational sources under license. Fine print often stares one in the face in such agreements only when it is too late. The technical consultants and the decision makers must have the specialised advice on international patent laws and should insist on specifications that are not simply proprietary brand names. The specified raw materials and the process control instruments must also be such as are readily available in the country. The association of the in-house industrial R&D or suitable Indian consultants is necessary even for deciding the purchase of know-how and the technology from abroad. West Germany allows support upto 65 per cent labour costs of the industrial R&D effort in that country. In India considerable tax concessions are given for building the industrial R&D facility within the industry.

3. Basic science

Most scientific progress is from the human quest for the understanding of nature. Some of the advances are made as a direct solution of issues raised during applications of science for example in making new equipment or instruments or materials. There is a continuous give and take between the basic and the applied science. Human progress through science therefore primarily rests on the progress in basic science. Every effort must be made that basic science continues to attract brilliant minds. There is the natural emphasis on progress in industry and the economic resources. In this preoccupation and the struggle for the production development part of the innovation chain often based on imported know-how, the importance for the future of basic science gets forgotten. Basic science however is the spring which eventually nourishes the development of a country. India is now fully alive to the planned support to basic science. International assistance for advanced work is available through international and inter-academy exchanges. University faculty jobs are being made more attractive in order to retain better minds. Certain teaching universities for agriculture or other applied science goals of interest to certain ministries other than that of education, feel that teaching and research are distinct and try to have separate staff earmarked for research work. This must be given up. Research work is a necessary component of university level teaching jobs. The subject does not come alive if the teacher is not engaged also in research effort. The current advanced experiments in basic science require very costly equipment e.g. the particle accelerators. For a relatively poor country, the scientific planners have to think harder and make do with the facilities that are possible. While Europe and USA are trying to study the decay of protons by billion dollar equipments, India is using the filtering of the required high energy protons from cosmic rays by going down in the Kolar gold mines using blocks of lead and relatively simpler equipment. Special facilities for basic research like radio telescopes, cyclotrons, nuclear reactors, instrumentation centres are being scattered all over the country for cooperative university research. Certain faculties are being selected from their experience and are allotted special funds for building up their groups as centres of advanced studies. Such funds are not hedged in by project completion dates and discontinuous support. There should always be encouragement to good workers who are spotted by various methods. India has now many prestigious fellowships, like the Nehru fellowships or INSA research professorships, UGC scheme of visiting professor etc so that scientists can carry out their work with minimum red tape. The attemps is also made to endow such fellowships in some cases with funds for research. It is in the long term interest of university departments to concentrate in certain specialisation so that they can attract better resources and can accomplish much more by joint efforts of a number of scientists working in the same area. If the effort is thinly distributed in many small areas, worthwhile results may not ensue. The current literature is full of unsolved problems, but the problems that are not significant or are involving only imitative work with changes in parameters cannot take us far on the road to progress. The direction and rate of discovery in basic science is unpredictable and society must not try to run science on a tight rein. One of the aims of science is to unify maximum number of observations under least number of assumptions and axioms. The boundaries between various science subjects like physics, chemistry, geophysics, materials science, genetics, environmental science, etc. are dwindling. Social scientists are also attempting the same relying on mathematical advances, statistics, computers, and field experiments and polls.

Whereas in the west for the past century private philanthopists had supported basic scientific research, they did not do much for the same in India. Technology advances through the efforts in connection with basic scientific research. Thus the spill over of technology to applied scientific work is the main economic return of basic science. The United States spent about U.S. dollars 6.4 billion on basic science in 1984 only. The government support to basic science is an example of centralised decentralisation, recognising the importance of local initiatives in scientific research. The planners and controllers fully realise that the research plans submitted in successful proposals need not subsequently be adhered to and deviations are natural. Funding will also depend on the publicity and publications of the group in question. Weinberg has proposed technological, scientific and social criteria. Scientist have to be intuitive as well as opportunistic. Since most research projects are interdisciplinary, besides the contributions of various specialists, the contributions of gifted individuals who have worked in more than a single discipline are highly valuable. In case of basic work the continuity over longer periods has to be ensured somehow e.g. by pre-project or post-project work often financed by the funds loosely placed at the disposal of directors of research groups. For work of applied or developmental nature, the timeliness and time horizons are important.

4. Project selection and evaluation

Vannever Bush has called science the endless frontier or a frontier at which the savants are always exploring. They manage their resources themselves under the system of peer review. The technical part of such work however is managed directly in terms of social and economic objectives. The holders of purse strings should realise the proportion of such basic work vis-a-vis applied scientific work which cannot be lower than 10 per cent in even the most bounded industrial in-house R&D group.

The peer review of project proposals and progress is universally accepted as a planning tool. In practice however the vulgar considerations of individual preferences based often on bias, colour the policy decisions. Science intensive output indicators like industrial innovation and growth, national defence capability, health, food, environment, energy, space capability etc. may govern selection of projects. National and international policies may be closely integrated with economic and social policies for optimum results. The planning involves anticipation of future needs and future technological progress. Attention must also be given to any long term adverse environmental or social effects. Advances in materials and communciations might lead to pollution by toxic chemicals, or traffic accidents. Prof. Brooks has mentioned the weighted consideration of technological opportunity compared to projected micro-economic impact to be necessary for selection of projects. A linked modelling programme has been created by the International Institute of Applied System Analysis at Trieste under the joint auspices of twelve nations. The U.S. Congress has set up an office of technology assessment. Feedback and monitoring in various programmes have also been started as these will improve technical planning. The circulation of technology across national boundaries, the speed of imitation and the diffusion of technologies are higher than ever. Multinational sharing of R&D priority work is not yet established.

Only feasible projects covered by the priority objectives of the organization are likely to get financial support under the constraint of limited funds. There must be good probability of success or of fall-out of new technology. The appraisal before adoption of results must re-examine the cost-effectiveness as well as the social costs, including the ultimate analysis of the objectives themselves. The funding organisations have their own priority objectives with assigned priority ranks. For each project that is under investigation, a merit rating can be calculated including the priority of the overall objective, the feasibility, the weighted cost-effectiveness, life of the resulting product, the size of the market, safety in transportation and operation and the ease of maintenance etc. For R&D work not leading to a product or process, the weighted cost-effectiveness is taken as unity. The evaluation at intermediate stages of the programme is useful for corrective revision or for termination of the project. Sometimes due to complacency, financial planning itself is considered as if the project has been accomplished. It is the results within the projected time frame that really matter and not just the appointment of contractors and making advance payments. In many such cases the equipment is not operated even once during the guarantee period for various reasons for lack of proper coordination and supervision. All along the progerssing of the project many choices or decisions are required. The science of decision making is the best guide for such choices in the face of uncertain future. Each alternative has a fractional probability associated with it (An alternative of certainty has the probability one). All such fractions get multiplied in the decision path and the final product of the fractions determines the best sequence of decisions. The creative decision makers have an intuitive feel for future states of nature or sudden upheavels in demand. It is on account of probabilistic nature of future that most decision makers do not place all eggs in one basket but have a basket of investment or diversification of actions and plurality of markets. Baye's probability theorem is the basis of combining additional experience with already existing probability estimates. Planners and decision makers must have command of scientific decision making tools.

Success of a planned measure rests on the amount of success in meeting the overall objectives. System analysis aims to optimise the cost-effectiveness or the rate efficiency but it has no control over the objectives themselves. Whether the objectives are properly chosen and how far the environmental and social impact of the objectives has been taken into account requires the expansion of the system analysis to 'ultimate' analysis. In the United States technical groups are functioning whose job is to criticize the plans on the basis of desirable value system.

By ultimate analysis is meant system analysis along with the validation (ethical or humanistic) of goals, inputs and fall-outs. Fascism had no use for ultimate analysis. Ultimate analysis would be the scientists' contribution to intergroup and international understanding. Such an analysis can forestall and re-channel social and economic mass-movements. Cybernetics and new technologies of knowledge could ease the growth of a self guiding society. Science also contributes to the development of human values by numerical experiments about evolution of the society under different value parameters. Scientific knowledge modifies and rationalises bias where it is not entirely eliminated. Prof. Weinberg has listed social merit, besides scientific and technological merits as the external crieteria of the validity of values, truth and unity being the internal criteria. Search of absolute values however is common to scientists and social scientists ; perhaps absolute values are also statistical composites offering different aspects to differently tuned intellects.

5. Transfer of Technology

Technology is the application of science to planning, to the choice and manipulatiôn of materials and equipment, like assembly, operations, quality control, marketing etc. for goal oriented processes. Technology is generated primarily in scientific and training institutions and is packaged in factories. Technological components have to be transferred initially to the engineers and technical managers and certain consultancy might spread the technological package to other entreprenuers in the same country or other countries. A developing country has to be pragmatic about the acquisition of technology. Technology is properly acquired and assimilated only when the recepient not only can use, but can also modify it and develop it for alternative materials and equipments. For such assimilation, highly trained and experienced engineers and scientists are required. India is now offering incentives to experienced Indians abroad to be consulants to Indian entrepreneurs and the public sector.

For economical and long range self-reliance capability, technology must be created within the country to the maximum extent. New technologies would be created in our universities and institutions. This needs patience and forward planning for longish time frames. The temptation however to import technology packages is great. The argument is for speedy self-sufficiency and quick addition to technology bank. So that such expectations are not belied, the indigenous capability should be sufficient to assimilate and further progress any technology. Otherwise quite often the accepted technology soon becomes out-of-date as did happen in the case of many technology packages obtained in the past directly by means of joint enterprises with transnationals.

For building of local technologies and the accumulation of data, engineering research, pilot plant experiments and experimental production are necessary. Unfortunately, adequate financial provision for such steps was not made in the planning of engineering education and of production. Engineering design data can be best collected by the planned allocation of a portion of manufacturing capacity to engineering experimentation and experimental production. This would be possible if the technical managers are fully alert for any ideas that suggest themselves towards cost reduction and materials and energy economy. Record of instrumented observations are necessary for such work dealing with the know-how. This would not be possible if there is indifference to obsolescence and the industry is sought to be run by employing only technicians picking up the minimum technical knowledge from the erecting and operating instructions. Thus research minded engineers should be available from the training institutions for work in factories. For proper transfer of technology from lab. to factory within the country, the ideal arrangement is to have the R&D cell within the industry. In the absence of adequate R&D in industry, an equally workable method would be to encourage the scientists and engineers in the research establishments to directly or indirect y assist industrial production and then to support such industries as consultants. The developing countries should take a leaf from the experience of developed countries and remove administrative and bureaucratic hurdles in the private practice of the scientists and engineers while in employment in university or public R&D institutions. Any secrecy and private technology can be secured by the clauses of agreements with R&D clients or the patent laws as well as the lead time automatically available with the sponsers. Reports of all sponsered R&D project must not be held as trade secrets beyond two years from the date of issue by the laboratory concerned. Scientists should also realize the inadvertant harm they may do to the development of the country by withholding their knowledge from entrepreneurs and the general public. There could be something like the Hippocratic oath for applied scientists and engineers. For a country of the size of India, there is every necessity for the spread of technology through the private practice of our scientists and engineers.

Technology transfer groups have now been set up by some important industries and departments primarily for assimilation of imported technologies and for export of technology packages by themselves or in association with other sources of know-how. Private engineering consultancy has also come up as a profession. Some scientists also banded together as volunteers in Science and tecnology assistance, but unfortunately, free consultancy is appreciated less. The entrepreneurs usually desire exclusive attention as by a private medical practitioner.

The agriculture is the major part of the private sector. The extension services by the agricultural universities and departments are firmly involved in transfer of technology to the farmers. Here also there is still scope for private effort. In 1820 Royal Agro-Horticultural Society was established in Calcutta and soon it had branches at major centres in British India. Upto 1866, such societies were the major vehicle for transferring technology and imported seeds to government farms and gardens as well as to rich farmers and planters in India. Private nurseries and seed farms are doing similar work now.

6. Evolution of Society through Science and Technology

Science and Technology have shown the means for a prosperous life for all. Upto now the prosperity was only for the few who rode herd over others. With the development of agriculture and industrial production, and the growth of humanist philosophies, democratic and economic equality of all is visible. The inequality in society seems to be built into it by the inherited and environmetal differences of individuals as well as almost universal laws of family based life and the rules for inheritence. Still the favouritism and the lack of equal opportunities must be eliminated to a large measure.

The means of communication are the general levellers of knowledge and therefore of power. The world has contracted, and neighbourhood extends across national frontiers. The nations are forming larger groups and there is the prospect of a genuine emergence of the United Nations. The international competition as well as cooperation are increasing for progress. The value system is shifting from the traditional to that of the scientific approach, that prepares the people to face the new world without superstition and magic.

The commitment of modern Indian polity of progress using science and technology is clear from the recently enunciated technology policy already referred to. The policy is fashioned to attain technological competence, and self-reliance for providing maximum gainful employment to all the strata of society with emphasis on jobs for women and the weaker sections. Technology gains will also usher in material and energy economy and provide tools for regeneration and husbanding of the environment.

10

CONCLUSION

1. Immediate Problems

We have studied the transformation of the Indian Society from the traditional to the modern one during the last century and a half. The introduction of modern science and technology and the pragmatic use of both private and state enterprise for increasing production and employment are the major characteristics of the transformation. The social goal of better living standards for the masses is intimately related to the assurance of external peace and absence of internal conflicts through the spread of friendly international relations and of scientific temper among the people.

The internal problems arise because of short range deals with political lobbies in the country against the spirit of the secular, democratic and socialist policies. The major political party is riding on the charismatic popularity of Gandhi, Nehru and Indira Gandhi which along with popular slogans wins them elections. But the country's development and the execution of the policies is entirely with the bureaucracy. There is no constitutional or traditional position of the political activists at the grass root level in the execution of the developmental policies. The political personalities exert their influence surreptitiously only for exacting favours or influencing decisions which cannot stand on merits and may be regarded as political interference in the functioning of the bureaucracy. Partly the situation arises because political organization in fact does not exist at the base level and has no role to play. The constitution requires speedy uplift of scheduled castes and scheduled tribes. In a vibrant revolutionary society, this should have happend in one or perhaps maximum two generations. The best results could be had by aiming special educational and training effort at the children in these backward communities. The active political cells would undertake to educate them and offer them new life at the expense of the community and the government and the transformation would be quicker than with the current efforts of offering them government service and promotions in service even when they cannot compete with others which only lowers the level of efficiency and creates obnoxious practices in the behaviour of these ill qualified officers as well as their colleagues from other castes.

The official policy is of non-discrimination on the basis of sex or religion. The position of women is not improving since many groups continue to practice customary law with impunity. The aim is to provide equal opportunity to all and also permit private enterprise and private profit and in addition to have a welfare state. All these desirable provisions must be made consistant with each other to the best possible extent. For the social balance with the private enterprise, the state must find resources for the spread of education and the scieniific temper and for municipal and other essential services. This allows taxes on production and a sales tax. The old fashioned graded taxes on personal incomes are incongruous with private profit and also the collection and enforcement is not worth the trouble. The individual income tax and road-side toll could safely be abolished and people allowed to live honestly than find ways to cheat. The use of revenue stamps for validation of receipts is a relic of imperial exploitation and is unethical.

Once a stable government can take appropriate monetary and fiscal measures and also happens to be controlling vast state enterprises and can control prices, attempts to collect individual income tax is hardly of any significance. The individuals' financial contributions must be realised through local units of the political party for local egalitarian measures. The voluntary constructive effort and supervision of execution of plans should be the natural function of social and political organization at the grass root level.

Private profit must include accumulation of wealth and investment in the future happiness of one's children and the cultivation of good things of life, along with possession and passing on of movable and immovable property. This may be allowed so far as equality of opportunity is not vitiated in the interest of the rich man's children through inheritence. The inheritence laws and the laws governing onwnership of property must be modified to absorb the Gandhian trusteeship theory. The government or a local estate administration must become the trustee for all privately owned means of production at the death of owners so that only a socially sound share accrues to the children and the rest goes to the national pool for direct or for lease use.

The latest modification gives equality to daughters with sons for inheriting property. The family however is patriarchical in most of the country, the daughter becomes a member of her husband's family and has no residential rights in her father's property. The custom requires dowry gifts from the father's family to the daughter at the time of marriage. Some rationalization is required. Parents' assets should be assessed at the time of a daughter's marriage and her share in rupee values be held in trust by the father of the girl for liquidation within a stipulated period in the interest of the girl who will not inherit any part of such property that accrues to the parents after the time of the daughter's marriage. This will do away with the problems connected with dowry and also with litigation regarding property between the two families later on especially when after one or two years, the girl usually gets integrated with her husband's family. This also will satisfy the complaint about the new inheritence laws from the agriculturists of the Punjab.

Secularism must not mean continuous attention to one only as a member of his distinct community and accord him favours or discrimination. The current policy in fact propagates caste and community based consideration. Secularism stands for equal consideration to all and filling all positions in considerations of merit and suitability alone. Many highly placcd individuals belonging to minorities often on retirement swear by communal labels primarily because they hope to propagate the favourable discrimination that had helped them earlier. Only in the most recent elections people seem to have voted independently of caste considerations. The system of vote banks in the pockets of caste elders was operating in the past.

2. Economic Growth

Continuous economic growth is needed for raising the living standards of the people. For increase in production the major ingredients are capital formation, trained labour force and advances in science and technology. In consumer oriented developed countries production of consumer goods is kept expanding by artificially creating demands for consumer goods by advertisement and encouraging emulation. For a country like India, where even essentials are not reaching the entire population, production of essential commodities and services has to be kept expanding. Perhaps we have to curtail the market for advertised goods and in place of providing consumer credit, we must have provision of credit through insurance companies for community services and for essential items like food, clothing and housing. Deficit financing can also be resorted to for national production and employment goals. For control over inflation, an ideological campaign for simplicity in life has to be waged.

In the past work has been considered as the caste mark of inferiority. A change of values is required to regard idleness as the symbol of inferiority. The entire policy structure should be work and production oriented. The political parties must be active at the grass root level and mobilize the local population for development. The preservation and improvement of the environment is a task which will always raise an echo in the Indian psyche. Each hamlet should have trash collection service and waste management planned and executed by itself without undue dependence on the bureaucracy.

3. Goal Oriented Action

The need is to guide resources to the most urgent ends. Inspite of Russia being only second best in production, she forged ahead in space science by pointed application of limited resources. The major obstacle to economic development is the crippling priority that must be given to diversion of resources for weapons of war and towards military preparedness. India has a stake in international peace and is a firm supporter of international cooperation, the United Nations and its agencies.

We must have price control so far as necessities are concerned and there should be less advertisement of consumer goods, and the money saved should be spent on propaganda for the simple life. For maximum decentralization, more distributed power resources especially the non-traditional like wind and water power from small scale generation, bio-gas and solar cells should be expanded. India could expand her development of land as well as ocean based materials and production of food. Best use of solar energy is in the production of agricultural or food items including the farming of fish.

Engineering research and Indian R&D cells should be closely linked with production even when bulk of the know-how is imported so that there is no stagnation in technology. Private practice by engineers and scientists in employment must became common and governed by common sense as is permitted to medical graduates.

There should be a thrust in the technology of maintenance and reliable life of equipment and materials and attention must be given to proper packaging, stock-piling and transportation of equipment and the upkeep of instruments. New technologies emerge primarily from basic science groups which must be strengthened. We must find resources to advance high technologies currently being developed elsewhere like bio-technology and automation.

4. Better Life

A better standard of life is less indicated by the possession of gadgets by a family but it is better indicated by the purposeful life spent by the family in self respect as well as social esteem. India has had the tradition of adoring a life style of simplicity, catholicity, and learning. The trend of resigning all art and music, philosophy and culture only to professionals has to be reversed by participative activity. Leisure will be increasingly available on account of automation for more efficient production and it has to be filled by better life style and not dcrepit idleness. As indicated earlier besides the economic and political steps so necessary for emphasis on increasing production, there should be conscious support of innovation and basic science. The new technologies emerge usually from basic science groups. The infrastructure of higher education in science, engineering and technology has to be strengthened. In this connection development of a common Indian link language for science with a common alphabet must be developed. Spread of scientific temper is basic to having an enlightened public that may not misuse the democratic rights guaranteed to them.

Apart from material welfare, the better life depends on work satisfaction and esteem of others or happy inter-personal relations. Freedom in the choice and place of work should be available to all. For material welfare of all during the development period of insufficiency and slow translation of planned development on the ground, ethics of simplicity and of work must be deliberately embraced. There is no room for violence in a free society and the superiority of non-violence and mildness must be understood. All isolated societies with abundance of food were always mild and non-violent and science and technology with promise of unlimited energy and gadgets and information, food and shelter is sure to usher in a future of abundance very shortly.

Human mind works at different planes and there is no clash between science and religion for personal salvation and solace. Only any beliefs that cause friction in the existing society and are only relics of different social conditions need to be submerged by scientific education, secularism and humanism. When one respects other person's freedom and faith, one is on the path of mutual cooperation and step by step to regional and universal understanding. Science permits an open mind and there is no room for fundamentalism or fanaticism.

Science offers a lasting frame of values based on observation, truth, reason and unity. Scientific attitude is tentative but total in its pursuit of truth. It is the scientific approach that held the Nazi soldiers guilty when they obeyed inhuman orders of Nazis in power. It is upto an educated man to discriminate and refuse to pursue goals that do not square with his ultimate value system.

BIBLIOGRAPHY

Bhatia, B.M. : *Famines in India*, Bombay, 1963.

Bose, D.M. *et al* : Science *A Concise History of Science in India*, INSA, New Delhi, 1971.

———, Science Policy in the Developing Nations, *Nature*, Vol. 1232, pp. 227-229.

———, The Republic of Science, Its Political and Economic Theory, *Minerva*, 1 (1), 54-73, 1962.

Brij Narain : *Indian Economic Life* : *Past and Present*, Lahore.

Bronowski, Jacob : *Science and Human Values*, Harper Torch Books, New York, 1984.

Brooks, Harvey Science, Technology and Human Values 7 (38), *Winter*, 1982, Princeton, MIT Press, pp. 13-32, 1983.

Bush Vanner *et al.* : *The Endles Frontier*, National Science Foundation, Washington, D.C., 1960.

Carroll James D. and Henry Nicholas : *Knowledge Management*, Public Administration Review, USA, pp. 567-602, 1975.

Drucker, Peter : Multinationals and Developing Countries—Myths and Realities, *Foreign Affairs*, 1982 (October) USIS, New Delhi, pp. 1-5.

———, Development : *Madras Development Series*, *Madras*, Feb. 1985, 17-136.

Dutt, R.C. : *The Economic History of India*, Vol. IX, 1903, (Indian Reprint), 1976.

Edie, James M. *et al.* : Russian Philosophy Vol. III, Univ. Tennesee Press, Knoxville, Ken. 1964.

Farkas, J. (Ed.) : Research : Gnostic and Social Aspects of Division of Labour and Cooperation in Research by Dietrich Wahl, *Sociology of Science*, Budapest, 1977.

Galbraith, John Kenneth : *Affluent Society*, Penguin, 1982.

———, Founders Address : *ICUS XIII*, Rev. Moon, Int. Cultural Foundation, New York, 1984.

Ghosh, Arun : Efficiency and Productivity of Indian Manufacturing Industry, 1397-1425, *Economic and Political Weekly*, Annual No. 19, 1984.

Ginzberg, V.L. : *Scientific Culture in the Contemporary World*, Scientia, Milano, 159-172.

———, Strategy of and for Science, Wayne Gunner, *ICUS XIII*, Paragon, New York, 1984.

Gierseh, Herbert (Ed.) : *Emerging Technologies, Consequences for Economic Growth, Structural Change and Employment, Symposium*, Inst. Welt-Wirtschaft and der Universtat, Kiel, pp. 328-377, 1981.

Gornay, Roderic : Human Agenda, The Guild of Tutors Press, Los Angeles, USA, 1979.

Gruber, W. and Marquis, A. : *Factors in the Transfer of Technology*, MIT Press, 1969.

Khanna, Sushil : Transnational Corporations and Technology Transfer, Indian Petrochemical Industry, *Economic and Political Weekly*, Vol. 19, pp. 1310—1340, 1984.

Koestler, Arthur : *Creation : Act of Creation*, Hutchinson, London, 1964.

Kuczynsk, Jansuz : *Universalism in Social Science and Culture*, The Search for a Global Ideology, *ICUS XIII*, Washington D.C., 1984.

Lacey, A.R. : *Modern Philosophy*, Routage and Kegan Paul, Boston, 1982.

Moore, John R. : The Technology Transfer between a Large Science Oriented and a Large Market Oriented Company, *The North American Rockwell Challenge*, 111-115, 1969.

Munshi, K.M. and Majumdar, R.C. : *The History and Culture of the Indian People—British Paramountcy and Indian Renaissance* Part II, Bombay, 1965.

Myrdal, Gunnar : The Transfer of Technology to Underdeveloped Countries, *Scientific American*, pp. 172-178, 1974.

Nanda, J.N. : R&D : Evolution and Planning of Defence R&D, *Proc. Symp.* R&D Management, pp. 1-19, Inst. System Analysis, New Delhi, 1977.

Nanda, J.N. : Fields Requiring R&D Funds, *Labdev J. Sc. Teach.* Vol. 8B, pp. 9-13, 1970.

NCST Panel *on Futurology* : *An Outlook for India's Future* (2000 A.D.) DST, New Delhi, 1-77, 1980.

Randhawa, M.S. : *History* : *History of Agriculture in India*, Vol. III, ICAR, 1982.

Skorov, G. : Transfer of Technology and New-Colonial Man-no

vering, *Strategic Digest*, pp. 56-67, Sept. 1972.

Sukhatma, P.V. (Ed.) : New coupts in Nutrition and their Application Maharashtra Academy of Culcutta and Services, Pune, 1983.

Tarlok Singh : *Literate Rural Youth as a Human Resource : Imperative for Planning*, Monthly Commentry on Indian Economic Conditions, Annual number, pp. 117-125, 1984.

Thomas, Howard : *Decision Theory and Manager*, Pitman, p. 137, 1937.

Verma, A.R. (Ed.) : Management and Role for R&D for Industry, *Symposium Summary and Recommendations*, INSA, 1980,

Weinberg, Alvin M. : *Criteria for Scientific Choice*, Minerva I and III, pp. 159-171 and 3—14, 1963.

Weinberg, Alvin M. : *Values in Science*, Paragon, New York, 1984.

Wigner, Eugene P. : Reflections on the Role and Purpose of Science, *ICUS XIII*, Paragon, New York, 1984.

Wilson, H.H. : *Moore Croft's Travels*, Asiatic Society, Calcutta, 1837.

———, Development of Irrigation in India, CWPC, New Delhi, 1965.

INDEX

ERRATA

Page		Line	Error
33		8 from bottom	Chiang
35		2 from top	many
42		11 ,, ,,	treaty
62		7 ,, ,,	technology
67		16 ,, ,,	nuclear
70		9 from bottom	cooperation
91		24 from top	own
95		3 from bottom	Position of women
102		11 from top	offering
110		5 ,, ,,	incapacitating
116	(i)	18 ,, ,,	thinkers
	(ii)	35 ,, ,,	provides
127		2 from top	encountered
135		12 ,, ,,	transcend